PAID TO BE YOU

VANESSA HALLICK

Elevate Your Mindset, Unleash Your Message &
Have It All Without Sacrifice

PRAISE FOR PAID TO BE YOU

"Reading Paid To Be You changed my entire perception of money (and beyond). I received this book at the exact right time— literally every single thing you mention that may happen as a sign of uplevel/growth was happening to me, in real time, as I read the book. I had been disconnected, distracted, scared I didn't know enough, reconsidering my goals... the list goes on. I'm so grateful I was reading this at that time, because I honestly just thought my life was about to fall apart. To re-frame my "symptoms" as growth and expansion made me excited about what was coming—and, to my delight and surprise, a huge career advancement came as I was reading this book. Thank you Vanessa, from the bottom of my heart, for sharing your downloads and your message with the world. You are a true light, and as I read and re-read, I continue to unveil layers of myself and my truth" — **EMILY DICKINSON**, Editor

"Through Vanessa's words, but more importantly her story and experience, she has given me permission to be me. That is the greatest gift one could ever receive. But she didn't stop there, she has infused science, psychology and spirituality in a way that truly guides you to completely shed your old patterns. The essence of this book is full permission to get paid to be you and live the life you (secretly) desire." — **ASHLEY-ANN PEREIRA**, The Studio Press

"I have been working with Vanessa and her work for over 2 years. The amount of gold nuggets, the amount of knowledge and gifts she passes on is amazing. She has taught me from the very start of our journey to speak my truth and be paid to do what I love; which is speaking on stage, assisting others to share their truth, and to break from the shackles of what holds people back in their lives. It has been an absolute pleasure to be a part of Vanessa's journey and have her inspire me daily to be in alignment with my soul's purpose. Without her and her mentorship, I don't know where I would be and how I could serve my clients, she has a special gift within and so much light to share. Her energy is divine. Enjoy this book as I have enjoyed this book too!" — **ALICIA ANN WADE**, International Life Coach of the Year 2020, International Best Selling Author 2020, Mentor, Key Note Speaker, President QCWA, Vice President Labor Party Hervey Bay

"Vanessa has been my coach for three weeks and in that time, I raised my prices from $500 to $5,000, signed up 12 soul students, decluttered my home, and started walking daily in nature. This process of honoring my highest self started with my business but ended up transforming my entire life. I'm beyond grateful to Vanessa and so excited to continue this beautiful journey with her!" — **ERIN WERLEY**, Bestselling Author of "I AM" , Quantum Energy Healer and Lightbringer

"Working with Vanessa has been pure magic. Before joining her supercharge program, I was playing it small in business and lacked the confidence to go big and embrace all of me. I've learnt I don't need to be an "expert" with all the qualifications in the world... me, my story and my energy is enough and I'm the expert of my life. When I embrace my authentic self, work with my human design, allow the crumble of the old and make decisions based on my next level self, magic happens. Thank you for guiding me and helping me to feel not only "enough", but bloody amazing and powerful." — **ANNA FRANKLIN**, Intuitive Healer & Empowerment Coach

"Well..where do I start! When I first started working with Vanessa I had no idea the huge impact that she was going to have on my life. Not only did she open up a new world for me in terms of business- that I truly can have it all- the abundant amount of success while having a balanced life but the most profound teaching that I still go back to is accepting all parts of me. I've never felt so comfortable speaking my truth which has allowed me to become a version of me that I didn't think was possible. Her words are like food to the soul and even though they can be triggering AF, they activate a part of you that needs to come alive. I'm so grateful that this beautiful human came into my life..exactly when I needed it most." — **MARYANN MOLOKU**, Intuitive Business Coach

"I took part in Vanessa's Unleash Yourself 10 day program in June. She helped me to work through some of my core limiting beliefs and face things I didn't really want to but needed to in order to grow. It was uncomfortable at times but also very liberating. One of the sessions Vanessa made us do a visualization exercise. It made me realise I had big dreams (bigger than I had before) that I was too scared to admit even to myself. I literally had tears rolling down my face and a big smile when I let these visions come through without pushing them away. Since then, I took the first step to make this dream come true, without any "grabby hands" and attaching any expectations, I am just going with the flow. This is a big step for me and start of a new journey I have never thought I would dare to embark on. Vanessa reminded me that I have my own special power and message that only I can pass on, which has become a sort of mantra in my business and personal life too. Vanessa's passion is contagious and empowering beyond your imagination. Thank you so much for all the wise words you have shared with us on that course. I loved every minute!" — **VIKTORIA GARBETT**, Twiddle – Love Of Food

"Vanessa and this book have not only been a breath of fresh air, but also like finding a true best friend. Only a best friend will call you out on your bullshit, that you're playing small and dulling your light. But does it with love and compassion, giving you the permission and space to slow down in this chaotic world to find clarity of your own path. Without

Vanessa, I'd still be stuck churning in what I think I'm "supposed to be", but now I'm building an empire on WHO I AM — and it's working, effortlessly. I have nothing but gratitude." — **KATRINA HUBBARD**, Branding That Banks

"'Paid To Be You' *is a game-changer if you're ready to really have it all. Vanessa is going to remind you how gorgeous you are and what you came here for. She'll activate your gifts & make you unstoppable. Such an honour to be a part of your beautiful journey."* — Your soul client & friend — **ANETA**, Business Coach

"I've never been more amazed at someone's desire to not only produce an extraordinary life for herself but equally as obsessed in helping others create it as well. Vanessa breaks all the "rules" and has created success in life HER way. And what I love the most about it is that she doesn't push her way onto others. She SHOWS them what is possible and then allows them to create their own roadmap. She's more than a business coach, she's someone that will change your life to the core. If you've been looking to learn from someone who has your best interest in mind, look no further... you've found Vanessa for a reason!" — **CHANTEL GATIEN**, Marketing & Scaling Expert For Coaches

"Vanessa is truly a light-worker. Her insights about the power of being truly authentic and creating a business that is aligned with your unique gifts are priceless. She is a thought leader when it comes to working through the shadows and limiting beliefs that hold you back from being your best self and living your most amazing life. Her book will guide you and your path to becoming your highest version of yourself and creating the business, impact and life you're dreaming of." — **KRISTIN HARTJES**, Business Mentor for Health Coaches

"Dear Vanessa, thank you for challenging me to get bolder, supporting me as I break open further and encouraging me to go deeper in uncovering my divine purpose. The path of a visionary entrepreneur is not for the faint hearted — which is probably why it is those of us born with a mighty heart who choose to listen to the call of the wild and follow the whisperings of our soul. While it may seem lovely and even terrifying at times, it doesn't have to be that way. Let Vanessa's strength, skills and magic guide, reassure and inspire you on the way to being paid to be you. Dulling down and hiding your light is so 'old paradigm'. This book will show you the 'why' but more importantly, the 'how' of stepping into your power, owning your gifts and healing your relationship to success and money. An exhilarating manual that teaches you that you get to have it all." — **ARYN GUINEY**, Brand Messaging & Copywriting Coach incorporating Embodiment and Somatic practices

PAID TO BE YOU

Elevate Your Mindset, Unleash Your Message &
Have It All Without Sacrifice

Cover Design by: Shawna Poliziani at Wolves and Roses Creative
Interior Design by: Fleck Creative
Edited by: The Studio Press
Publishing Assistance: The Studio Press

ISBN: 978-0-620-99151-3 (paperback)
ISBN: 978-0-620-96058-8 (e-book)

To contact the author, visit: *www.vanessahallick.com*

This book is dedicated to my incredible soulmate, Shaun. My business partner, lover and guide. My deepest teacher, mirror and healer.

Thank you for always supporting me, guiding me, and believing in me. For being there at the lowest points of anxiety, burnout and suicidal thoughts. For always guiding me home to my truth.

We couldn't be more different, and I love how through this polarity, we learn and grow from each other. You've taught me to slow down and embrace the present moment. To look at the birds and animals on our many hikes. You've taught me that I can do anything, and that no dream is too big.

You've listened to my moaning, drama, emotional rollercoasters, and judgements; you've helped me transmute it, and guided me toward the awareness I've gained to be able to write this book.

To 13 years together and a lifetime to go.

I love you. I am grateful for you. Together we can create anything.

YOUR INTENTION

Record what you hope to get out of this book as you embark on your journey through it's pages:

CONTENTS

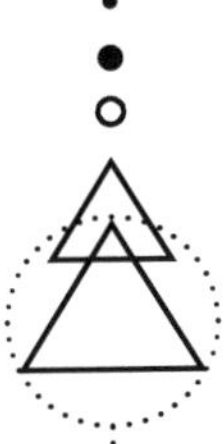

Paid To Be You: Introduction

Writing a book shakes you to the core. It unravels your deepest fears, your darkest memories, and uncovers *a lot* of things that you didn't realise about yourself.

That is what this book is all about.

It's about cracking yourself open and allowing yourself to be seen: I'm talking about nude-on-the-internet, unapologetic, shouting-out-whatever-you-are-called-to-share, and doing whatever turns *you* on. It's about learning to be fully seen and heard with zero fucks given.

This book is about saying goodbye to being timid, to dipping your toes in, and to living half-in-half-out. None of that. Not anymore.

This book is about committing to radical self-honesty. It's time to admit to yourself what you *really* want, how you *really* want to feel, and what you *really* want to create in this world. No holding back, no holds barred.

Your soul is calling you to listen, to answer, and to rise up and lead. And I am here to help you do it.

I started my coaching business in 2015, and have since worked with thousands of female entrepreneurs. The most common mistake I see women making is dimming their (bright) lights and hiding who they really are.

If you're here, I'll assume that you can relate. I'll assume that you have a deep desire to be seen, heard and valued for being *you.* I'll assume that you're ready for change. It's important to note that it's not your fault for acting small. You've been conditioned that way, and now it's time to take your power back and break free of those stories and roles you've been playing for far too long.

This is what I know to be true: there is nothing more powerful and magnetic than you owning your truth, honouring your desires and following what truly lights you up.

What lights you up, lights up the world.

Read that again. Holding back your light does a disservice to the world. We have profound and unique gifts to share, and yes, that includes yours.

FACING YOUR DEEP-ROOTED FEAR

How does it feel in your body knowing that you have everything within you *right now* to create whatever you want?

Perhaps you're afraid of your power and bigness. Perhaps you're afraid of being too much, too loud, too ambitious, or too outspoken. You've been living the watered down, good-girl version of yourself. In that version, you break a few rules, but you stay (mostly) within the confines of what is expected of you so that you're loved, accepted and valued.

I get it—I was afraid for a long time, too. I ran far away from my truth until I wasn't able to any longer. I wanted so badly to be loved by everyone that I was a chronic people-pleaser with a serious lack of boundaries. It was a recipe for burnout.

I tried to play it safe: I got good grades, went to university, and climbed the corporate ladder in an unfulfilling job while my personal life crumbled. Binge-eating, meaningless sex, and a lot of shopping were the destructive ways I knew how to cope.

When I finally quit my corporate job and started my business, things didn't magically change. (It's kind of like thinking that losing weight will make you happy. It never happens that way.) Making money works the same way—millions of dollars won't automatically buy you happiness, fulfillment or joy. In fact, as you'll read later, money only amplifies what is already within you. Deep down I knew I was on the right path, and was made for more. The journey was the beginning of a deep excavation and a lot of excruciating discomfort to let go of all that I thought I knew about myself and transform into who I was meant to be.

At first, getting out of my corporate job was my mission. After achieving that, I wanted to make enough money to have Shaun—my partner—join me in the business. Once I made that happen, I wanted to have a million-dollar year.

In 2018, I wrote in my journal how I was going to become the 7-figure-a-year version of myself. This is what I decided to do:

- Invest $60K cash in a high level coach
- Hire a publicist
- Show more of my life in Bali
- Have a bigger team
- Have an automated webinar funnel and a massive ad spend

An array of **do more**, **invest more** and **pretend more** from a deep wound of not feeling good enough.

Instead of a 7-figure year, I got burnout, severe anxiety attacks, and suicidal thoughts. It was a frightening time in my life and not at all what I expected. I had hit my rock bottom.

My plans of investing and expanding weren't fundamentally bad, but I was doing them from the energy of *needing* to make a million dollars to satisfy my ego. I believed that if I had a 7-figure year, I would feel whole, worthy, and happy. I'd be seen as the go-to coach in the industry. *Then* I wouldn't feel like an imposter. Meanwhile, my soul was crying out for *more*.

As I crashed, clients started leaving. Even now, years later, as I think about that time I can feel fear and guilt present in my body. However, looking back, this was exactly what I needed to awaken to my truth and to be sitting here today writing this book.

You always get what you need, not necessarily what you want.

This book is something I have been deeply guided to share with you. It's part of my life's mission, one that I promised I would fulfill at my darkest moments.

This is what I wrote at my rock bottom:

"If you give me the strength to heal and continue my business, I vow to commit my life to helping others awaken to their truth and give back freely to those less fortunate. I know I'm meant to have an overflow of money to be able to do that and I'm committed to this mission and purpose."

That brought tears to my eyes.

A woman with a mission and purpose who is willing to claim what she wants and takes the aligned action is unstoppable.

Life is a crazy journey. Just when you think you have it all figured out, you're asked to go deeper within and share more of yourself. I've learned to appreciate this as part of choosing this path in life. We are here to evolve and grow, after all.

It's time to get comfortable with the uncomfortable.

UNAPOLOGETICALLY PAID TO BE YOU

Being paid to be you is often uncomfortable and inconvenient. It's not an easy road. However, the life of being fully guided, supported and trusting your bigger reason, is *the most* incredible gift. It sets you free from the shackles of conformity. It gives you permission to feel at the depths you've never felt and to be alive at a level that is difficult to describe in words. I can't wait for you to feel that feeling.

Look: I know you crave more. Maybe you lie awake at night wondering how you can make a bigger impact. Maybe you desire

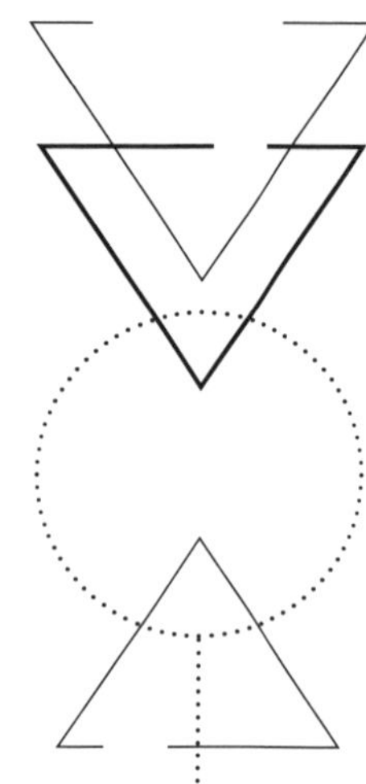

A woman with a mission and purpose who is willing to claim what she wants and takes the aligned action is unstoppable.

a ripple effect of change in the world. Maybe you're questioning the point, thinking:

- ▷ Who am I to do this work?
- ▷ Who am I to think I can create this change?
- ▷ Who am I to share my experience?

If you've asked yourself these questions, you're not alone. Your soul knows. You're here for bigger things.

Who are you not to?

Paid To Be You is my journey from being paid for the work I was doing, to having a love affair with the work I get to do/create/embody from my soul.

I thought that working hard had to come with sacrifice, 14-hour work days, difficult clients, hard conversations around money, and taking on more responsibility. I thought that building a business had to be hard, filled with struggle and sleepless nights.

This reality exists and it is available for you if you choose it. Sadly, most people do. Most feel that this is the only option available to them.

However, within these pages, I am going to present an alternative reality. An option that is also available to you, should you choose to explore it.

The reality I will present is a reality where you get paid to do what you love and work with the most incredible clients that are grateful for you and excited to pay you anything you charge. This is a reality where you feel energized and radiant, where you speak your truth and share the message that is coming through you.

The money? Taken care of.

Feeling amazing in your body? Totally taken care of.

Your ideal relationship? It's yours.

Anything you want is provided, as long as you honour who you are and follow through on the actions you're guided to take.

That is my reality. I am paid to be me. I work with soul clients who love to pay me and are making massive moves in the world, just by being themselves.

Are you ready to be courageous, audacious and go against the grain to claim that you get to have it all, on your terms, without sacrifice? The first step is choosing, with faith, that this is available to you.

Paid To Be You is not for the faint of heart. This book is going to trigger you as you release layers, and it will likely make you question most of what you've been taught so that you can come back to your inner knowing. It won't be rainbows and unicorns. It will take you back to who you really are, and ignite the magnificence that you came here with. My hope is that this book jolts you, awakens you, and disrupts your current paradigm so that you can create what you are *really* meant for in this lifetime. We can't create a different reality with our current thinking and actions.

I know you're ready to transform. Say it with me: I am ready to be paid to be me!

You were born whole, perfect, with a mission, a purpose and unique gifts. Now is the time to remember. You wouldn't be here if this wasn't meant for you.

I'm known for my loving smackdowns, I am a bulls*** detector, and my clients go on to create incredible things because of newfound beliefs they discover while working with me. You can't *not* transform in my vortex.

I know I can't be there physically with you, but know that I'm there with you in spirit, in energy, and guiding you each step of the way to your truth.

Remember, everything is energy and energy is everything. I believe that by reading this book, embracing the stories of other women who are being paid to be themselves and doing the exercises that feel aligned, you will experience incredible shifts and miracles in your life. Some things will continue to shift as you practice a new way of thinking, believing and showing up in the world. As you continue to expand your beliefs around what is possible for you, you'll remember the truth that infinite possibilities exist for you.

You are the conscious creator of your reality.

You get to choose the path of struggle, exhaustion and sacrifice—but radiance, joy and devotion to your purpose is equally available to you.

With every page you read, my hope is that you start to remember, call back, own and activate the power that has been within you all along. To feel untamed, unhinged and at times... naughty.

To make you squeal with delight and blush while you deepen into your magnificence.

You can read the book in its entirety, or dip into sections. Come back to chapters whenever and however you desire. This is your playbook, your journey, and your adventure. (I know you're a radical rule breaker—welcome to my world!)

What you see in your reality today may radically shift in the next couple of weeks. When our inner world transforms, this is reflected in our outer reality. You will evolve, grow and shift. Your perception of who you are and who you are meant to be will change.

True inner peace has been something I always desired, but I had distorted expectations of it. At first, I thought inner peace was about eradicating hardships from my life. Now I know that true inner peace comes from the deep knowing that you can handle whatever comes your way. It comes from knowing that you are far more resilient, powerful and resourceful than you could ever imagine. That you get to honour every emotion and every divine cycle of your life. You get to navigate the human experience with passion.

The next level in your business is not about a number. It's not about a 7-figure this or a multi-million-dollar that. It's how you redefine your standards, boundaries, and emotional intelligence so that you can be the woman who can hold wealth without sacrifice. It is wholly honouring your soul, speaking your truth, and being unapologetically you.

Remember: when you rise up, you give others permission to do the same.

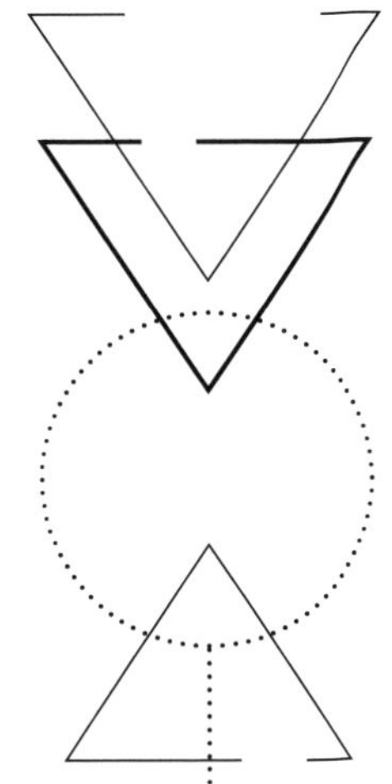

When you rise up, you give others permission to do the same.

I'm not here for shallow living, and if you're here I know neither are you. You know that you're here to evolve, to grow, to rise up, and to lead a movement.

This is not another book reminding you of all the things that are wrong or need fixing. It's not another book telling you how much more you have to, must and should do. It is a reminder of how powerful and limitless you truly are—just as you *already* are.

You're loved, you're worthy, and you're capable of creating whatever you want in this lifetime.

Let's excavate the unhelpful beliefs. Stay with me, as I'll be providing a new way of thinking, being and living. Some of it may feel outrageous and a lot will feel uncomfortable, but my hope is that you'll love this new way a lot more and start to adopt it as your own.

Let's create a ripple effect of change in the world, together.

Vanessa xox

ENERGETIC ACTIVATION

For the audio of this activation visit: www.vanessahallick.com/paid

Remember, you get to create your reality. You are a powerful creator. You have everything you need within you now, to be paid to be you. It is time to remember who you are and call back the disenfranchised parts of you.

When you slow down enough to listen and connect to your soul, you'll be amazed at the miracle and gift you truly are in the world. There is nothing wrong with you.

Let's begin this magical journey together—this journey of uncovering your truth, remembering who you are, and following your soul's calling so that you can create the ripple effect of change in the world that you are born to make.

I want you to go to a beautiful, quiet space where you can enjoy this process of unleashing, uncovering and unlocking parts of you that you've forgotten and neglected.

I want you to remember that you are not broken and you're not in need of fixing. You don't have huge blocks stopping you from your brilliance. You simply have forgotten your magic, forgotten the power that resides in you, and forgotten how incredible you truly are.

This book is a remembrance: a remembrance of your truth, a remembrance of your divine gifts, a remembrance of who you came here to be. A reconnecting to your path, your destiny, and your soul's calling.

Together we're going to journey into the depths of your soul. We're going to uncover your truth, we're going to unleash parts of you that you've been ashamed, upset, and suppressed, so that you can be free to do what you're meant to.

Your unique voice matters, your message matters, and your signature methodology in the world matters. You are infinitely guided, supported and protected on this journey.

Now, I want you to take four deep breaths in. Hold for the count of four, and as you exhale for the count of eight (4-4-8), I want you to feel anything that you've been holding onto—anything that has stopped you from your brilliance. Visualise this melting off your body.

*Take another deep breath in, hold for four, and release slowly for eight. And on that exhale, allow yourself to release anything that no longer serves you. *deep exhale**

Now, start to visualise a beautiful white light emanating from the base of your spine. See it as it circles in a figure eight, as it balances the masculine and feminine energy within you. As you move the white light from the base of your spine, you feel your root chakra aligning and moving the energy in a clockwise direction. As you move the energy into your sacral center (2 fingers below your belly button) and you heal your sacral center.

And as you move that energy just above your belly button into your solar plexus, the seat of your personal power, it starts to activate. You say: I call back my power, I call back my power. Follow that energy up in the figure eight as you balance the masculine and feminine energy, as you integrate all parts of you and you move energy now into your heart center. As your heart center starts to open and expand, allow and receive.

And as you move that energy now into your throat center, you feel an opening—a deep opening.

As you start to speak your truth, as you start to share your gifts with the world, and you are being paid to be unapologetically you. And now move that energy in a figure eight to your third eye, between your eyebrows, and just allow yourself to roll your eyes back and to start to activate that energy within your third eye and as you move that energy through your forehead, just above your head to your crown chakra and move that energy back down in the figure eight from your crown chakra to your third eye, to your throat center, to your heart center to your solar plexus, to your sacral center to your root chakra.

As you feel yourself start to activate, I want you to start to visualise the life that you desire. What are you wearing? How are you showing up? What are you creating? Remembering that your subconscious knows everything that you desire. Your soul knows exactly what you're meant for.

I want you now to visualise a flower opening at your heart center and allow that flower to open. At the center of that flower is a golden ball. Your soul holds your past, present, future and follows a golden thread from your soul up to the heavens, up to the Universe to your spirit guides. I want you now just to deepen that vision, as you feel totally connected to source energy, as you feel so connected to what you're here to do. I want you to feel that energy now of the certainty of your vision. What does success really look like for you? How does it feel in your body?

What clients do you really want to work with? How many clients do you desire to bring into your business? What support do you need from the physical realm—from the spiritual realm? And if you knew that you were infinitely supported, is there anything that you need to release now? And as you allow yourself to start to remember and uncover your truth, knowing you're always guided and protected, I want you to feel into that certainty that you have a purpose, that you have a divine destiny, that you are here for a reason.

I want you to feel into a space of faith and surrender, knowing that this book will guide you, will support you and will help you activate parts of you that you've forgotten and lost. And as you remember—as you return home to your truth—you remember you are gifted, you are more than enough, you are loved, you are wild, you are free, you are female.

And as you allow this moment—as you connect into that truth—you know that you're reading this book for a reason and that my voice, my message, my energy is guiding you, holding you, and leading you to your truth.

When good, beautiful, visionaries make a lot of money, they can do great things in the world. It is time to lead, rise and answer the call of your soul.

This book is a remembrance, an activation of your truth, a realignment with your wealthy self. An activation of your truth that you do get paid to be the best version of you. I want you to feel that energy: how does it feel in your body to be protected and guided? How does it feel in your pussy to be reunited with your turn on?

I want you to allow yourself now to close the old chapter of your book—the chapter of your life—and as you open a new chapter, I want you now to write on a clear page and to see for yourself: what is your future? What does your vision really look like? What do you really desire in love, life, health and happiness? Visualise a blank page where everything that is channeling through you now is writing itself in the book. What message are you receiving? What is the information that you're being guided to? Allow that information as a channel, as the messenger, to come through you now. Let that information fill that new page, and as you allow yourself to let that information channel through you, I want you to go back to your heart center and I want you to close the flower. Visualise the golden ball being reintegrated into your body.

I want you to visualise your spirit coming back into your physical body. Mind, body, soul, spirit integration as you feel whole, as you feel healed, as you feel integrated, as you feel ready to step boldly into the next level version of you where you rise, where you lead, where you provoke a new consciousness.

Where you create a ripple effect of change.

And as you open your eyes, I want you to take out a journal and I want you to write what you saw on the page. I want you to write anything you saw in this visualisation, how it felt to be in absolute certainty. I want you to remember that you're guided, you're protected and you are a vessel for change.

Write about what came up during the activation.

PREPARING TO BE PAID TO BE YOU

If you can see it in your mind, you can create it in your reality.

Before we dive in, let's do a check-in. Write down the answers somewhere that you can refer back to later.

▷ **On a scale of 1–10, how confident do you feel about being paid to be you?**

My definition: Being paid to be you is receiving divine compensation for your innate gifts, skills and experience. It is about speaking your truth, being unapologetically you, selling what you want in the way that you want and attracting soul clients that you adore working with, all the while feeling turned on, radiant and free.

- What is not currently aligned?

    E.g. I am not selling my aligned program, I am not speaking my truth, I am not attracting soul clients with ease.

- What thoughts, beliefs and fears do you have about being paid to be you?

- What are you telling yourself you are going to need to sacrifice if you follow this path?

Put your hand on your heart and close your eyes. Breathe slow, deep, and gently.

Ask: "Universe, what guidance do you have for me here about being paid to be me?"

Be still and listen for the still, small voice inside. What guidance is coming forward? Write down the guidance you receive.

Set a powerful intention right now of how you want to feel, what you want to shift and what you're willing to release and create to be paid to be you.

Let's begin this journey.

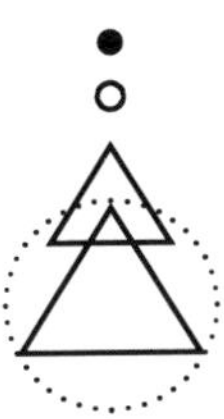

chapter 1

From Failure To Making Millions (Without Sacrifice)

In September 2018, I hit rock bottom.

Wanting to cut my throat and wrists with the kitchen knife.

I wasn't sleeping or eating. I would spend my mornings walking around the kitchen and pool wondering if I had the strength to end my life.

On paper, I had it all. I had taken the brave leap to leave my unsatisfying corporate job, and I had created a lucrative business I was proud of. I had an incredible fiancé, a luxurious life in Bali, and I was featured in *Forbes, Red Online, FT Advisor,* and other major publications. I had six-figures in savings and was making millions online (without a sales team). I was travelling the world with my fiancé, Shaun, staying in luxury five-star hotels in Singapore, Sri Lanka, and Malaysia, and creating transformations in the lives of our clients. But on the inside, I was a train wreck. I was miserable and filled with fears. I had everything I thought I wanted, but the fear of losing my business and being seen as a failure haunted me.

Life was filled with a colourful array of drama, self-sabotage, worry and exhaustion.

- ▷ If you're not exhausted, are you doing enough?
- ▷ If you don't feel pain or struggle, are you doing it right?

These were the unconscious thoughts I had on replay.

What I now know to be true is that I was meant to experience burnout and suicidal thoughts so that I could break the unworthiness paradigm. This book is my journey of transformation that has allowed me to share this message with you. Success is not external and you can experience abundance in all areas of your life, without sacrifice.

It is my mission and purpose on this planet to help you see that *success isn't in what you acquire and it's not external to you.* Success is about cultivating and creating deep inner acceptance, truth and happiness. From this space, we have the ability to receive what is meant for us and enjoy living the human experience in the way we are made to, without sacrificing our health or relationships. **One shoe does not have to fall.**

The more I spoke to entrepreneurs, the more I heard a similar story. They were riddled with guilt, shame and fear. They had experienced burnout from feeling the need to push themselves to do things and prove their worthiness because of a deep wound that told them they weren't good enough.

They told me that 6-figure burnout was common. The more they acquired material success, the more the fear mounted.

As I write this, I am brought to tears. We sacrifice ourselves to be something we were never meant to be because of society, our parents and our childhood conditioning.

We create expectations of how our life *should* be and what we *should* do, perpetually comparing ourselves to others. Believing so deeply that our self-worth and lovability is in what we do, acquire and create. That the amount in our bank account determines who we are as people. It doesn't.

You are worthy and brilliant as you sit there now.

When you start to embrace the fact that you are incredible and worthy as you are, you get to harness the fact that your mess is your message, and that anything you go through and heal from makes you a better healer, coach, visionary and leader.

It makes you better equipped to support your clients. Your community will have similar wounds to you, so when you go through something, you are able to see these patterns in others and support them.

You chose this path and the lessons in this lifetime, so it's time to drop the guilt, shame and fears around sharing all parts of you. Your message can shift those around you if you allow yourself to see the gift in life's ruptures. Accepting who you are—wholly and fully—is the key to doing anything you want in this lifetime. You're stronger and more resilient than you know. Trust me.

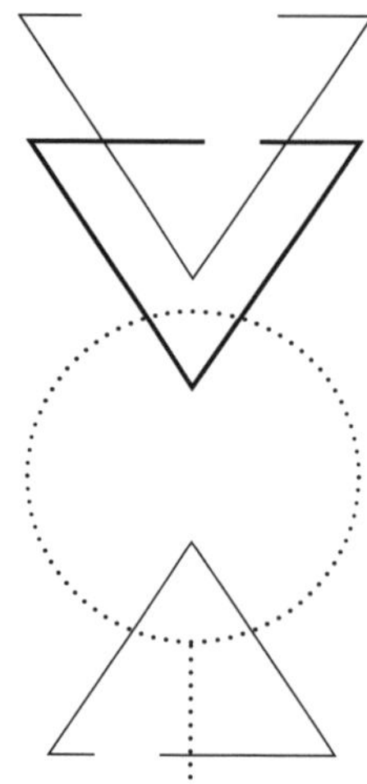

You are worthy and brilliant as you sit there now.

BUSINESS AND MENTAL HEALTH

Mental health issues are real and aren't reserved for the successful, lazy, poor or rich. It can affect anyone at any time. Creating rituals and routines to support your mental health as you grow your business is *so* important. It will help you expand your energetic capacity to receive more. It is a win-win.

Instead of constantly trying to do more, let's go deeper into devotion, ritual and deeply honouring yourself.

Your brain can be rewired. Trauma can be released and you can feel energised, vibrant and happy. Stress, taking on responsibility for others, and trying to fix from a space of not feeling good enough will have serious repercussions. Not feeling good enough and pushing and proving from this space wreaks havoc on your immune and nervous system. If your nervous system is maxed out, it will naturally stop you from taking on more clients to protect you.

Simply put: to see your business soar, it's essential to do the inner work to understand your truth! When you realise you are already whole and magnificent as you are—you are simply remembering with each new awareness.

Life can get infinitely better when you own your shadow self, embrace your uniqueness, feel your feelings, and honour your natural rhythms. When you commit to this journey, you will remember your wholeness (your natural state where you receive what is meant for you with ease). When you choose and decide what you are available for, when you understand your patterns, release the past and take action from this space, getting paid to be you is natural and effortless. You are meant to be divinely compensated for your unique gifts.

Business can be the *most* incredible experience and it doesn't have to come with unnecessary stress and burnout. Fun, pleasure and happiness are needed (essential, actually) when you have your own business.

The more fun and pleasure you allow, the more impact and income you make. When we are in a state of pleasure and arousal, we shift our vibration and frequency, attracting more of what we want into our lives.

Just like there is no point faking an orgasm, you can't fake pleasure and joy in your business. When you are tapped into your soul's authentic truth, there will be no forcing; only feeling. You'll be in divine flow, and you will know that you are guided, supported, and one with source energy. Sounds pretty great, doesn't it?

Success and being paid to be you is an inside job that requires taking spiritually-aligned actions. It's a return to love. A return to the magic that resides within you. When the doing becomes an extension of your most fully expressed self, true magic and miracles occur. Making money comes as easily as breathing; we expect money to show up and we have faith that we are always taken care of.

UNDERSTAND YOUR PAST TO EMBRACE YOUR PRESENT

There is no one on this planet who hasn't experienced some form of trauma. In order to understand who we truly are, we need to understand our patterns, habits and conditioning. It isn't about rehashing, blaming or being the victim. It's about recognising and questioning your current beliefs to uncover your truth and to be conscious of what is happening in your life.

- ▷ Where did you forget your magic?
- ▷ When did you start to think you weren't incredible as you are?

Before I dive into my past, I just want to put a disclaimer here for my mom and dad: I love them both dearly, and I am so grateful for the support, opportunities, and love they have provided me. Although they had their moments of fear when I left my "safe" corporate job, they have never doubted me. For that, I am eternally grateful. I am also *so* proud of how much they have grown with the conditioning and trauma they had, and continue to evolve and support my big vision.

Like you, the beliefs I formed in my childhood impacted my life until I was willing to unlearn them and reclaim my magic. I grew up on a farm in a small town in Knysna, South Africa, where I've since moved back to. I have two brothers—one older (Michael) and one younger (Sean)—and a sister (Jeneé) who is two years older than me. My parents had four children in just over five years! My father had mental health issues when I was younger, which led to fear and unpredictability in the household. To cope with this reality, we were taught to "get on with it."

Getting on with it meant that when we were sick, feeling emotional, or when life felt difficult, we were taught to be tough and move past it. It created a fierce resilience and instilled a go-getter attitude in me. Showing any signs of "weakness" (like being ill, sad or angry) was frowned upon. We were told that we couldn't be weak like *other people.* This created a lot of separation from others and a tribal mentality. The Hallicks were the leaders and other people were sheep following the crowd. *Getting on with it* helped us move forward and stay focused on getting through school and achieving at sports.

We were never sure what we would come home to. I never knew what fun was, or what kind of activities would make me happy. I was in survival mode dealing with severe anxiety and trichotillomania*;* a fancy word for obsessively pulling out my hair.

On the flip side, my mom taught me to look for solutions instead of focusing on the problem. I was also blessed with the belief that anything is possible, and that I didn't have to settle. Being a leader was deeply programmed into me, although the way I viewed it and others needed to shift.

I spent a lot of my childhood trying to be the best because of my deep rooted fear that I wasn't good enough. Growing up, we were told that in order to be successful or make a lot of money we'd have to be an accountant or lawyer. It was deeply ingrained that anything else would not meet the expectations and we wouldn't amount to much. We were told to work hard so that we could then enjoy our retirement.

Oh, how times have changed.

Throughout my childhood and early adult life, I played it safe and did what I thought I should do to achieve this idea of success that was instilled by my father. My plan was to go to university, get good grades, secure a job, climb the corporate ladder, and retire. I dimmed my light so that I could be loved, seen and accepted. I created a mask of who I thought I needed to be. To the outside world, I was Little Ness—cute and quiet. Behind the scenes, I was Messy Ness. Little Ness helped me achieve the grades, promotions, and ultimately, a thriving business. But she was *stressed*. She was focused on pleasing others. She thought that the key to feeling good enough was through achievements. However, her tantrums, anxiety and disordered binge eating were all signs of destructive behaviour.

I was living my life out of alignment.

Later in life, this led to being on a never-ending treadmill, simply making money to survive.

Is this it? Isn't there more to life than this?

THE JOURNEY TO BEING PAID TO BE ME

On my 30th Birthday—November 19, 2014, to be exact—instead of celebrating, I spent the day in tears. My acne was horrible, I had no energy, and I couldn't find meaning in my life. I promised myself that I would make a change, but I had no idea what that would look like.

Around this time, the idea of coaching had started to catch my attention. I knew I was passionate about helping people and had an energy that often led people to come to me for encouragement. I had a friend who was looking for a life coach, and she told me that I would be amazing at it. I was working in Human Resources at the time, but this excited me. I knew that my own coaching business was something that actually lit me up.

We didn't work together in that capacity, but it started my research. I had a newfound enthusiasm for the opportunity to start my own coaching business (without a boss and an organisation that wasn't aligned to my values). The bonus was that I could work from anywhere.

In January 2015, I decided to take the leap and build my coaching business while still in my HR job. After 10 years in my HR career, I realised that I loved helping others fulfill their fullest potential and create joy in their life and career. Unfortunately with HR, I also had to deal with a lot of disciplinary hearings, which I hated.

In March 2015, the maternity leave I was covering came to an end and I made the decision to focus solely on my business. Unfortunately, I soon realised that working tirelessly on my website, having professional photos, and creating social media pages was not enough to get paying clients. I partnered with a friend and worked with some of her clients, earning $25/hour. That wasn't going to pay the bills, but with every client I worked with, I came alive. I witnessed clients creating powerful shifts between sessions and I knew that this was what I was meant to do.

The problem was that I lacked confidence to charge more, I didn't know how to market myself effectively, and was selling one-off sessions. It was not a sustainable business model. I was too afraid to hire a business coach to support me because I was terrified to spend the savings I had. I ended up struggling for three months.

It was time to get back to a corporate job and give up on my failed business. I pulled myself to interviews and landed another job that I hated. This time I made it a total of three days before leaving in tears. It was clear that corporate life was *not* for me.

Then more than ever, I knew I had to make it work. I couldn't continue trying to fit into a mould, that wasn't for me. *I had to make it happen.* I was meant for it.

In June 2015, I hired a business coach. I realised that I could make money back, but I couldn't get my time back. I stayed in my tear-inducing HR job and stuck it out to support myself while focusing my off-time on building my business. I connected daily to my bigger vision and why I wanted to do this work. I believed it wholeheartedly. It was the only option.

A woman that sets a powerful intention and believes it's so...will make it happen.

On November 29, 2015, I handed in my one month's notice. I made $12,532 that month in my business, while working my corporate job. I went from charging $25 to $1500 for my 90-day one-on-one program. Now I charge multiple 5-figures to work one-on-one with me.

I finally had a business. It was real.

In the first year, I was building my business and working full time. There were a lot of sacrifices. My relationship suffered; Shaun and I almost went our separate ways. It had been a consistent pattern of sacrifice, exhaustion, anxiety and one shoe always falling.

With everything else in my life feeling like it was crumbling as my business started to thrive, I realised that change was needed. There was a glimmer of belief and inner knowing that I truly could have it all.

In September 2016, we moved to Bali. Shaun retired from his corporate job, and off we went. The business wasn't replacing both of our corporate incomes, but Shaun was sick of his corporate finance job and I was itching for an adventure. We had no idea what to expect, but we packed our bags.

Bali led me to deepen my spiritual path and connect with my intuition. It also brought the gift of burnout! This led me to a journey of healing myself, of getting support by shifting my beliefs around my worthiness and training in NLP, Reiki, Human Design, Breathwork, Quantum Healing, Shadow work, and more.

It was my invitation to redefine success and create abundance in all areas, *without* sacrifice.

When we are in a space of overflow of wealth, happiness and love, those around us shift much faster. Your energy and being all of you has the potential to transform others.

I now have made millions of dollars doing my soul's work. I get paid to be unapologetically me.

You are a divine, magnificent being. You are not broken or in need of fixing. You came to this world perfectly *you*, with the gifts, knowledge and DNA for *your version* of success. You have a soul contract to fulfill in this world with your unique gifts, and when you share your truth and sell in the way you are guided to, you will be divinely compensated. Love is money and money is love. It is not the root of all evil.

Success is about returning home and remembering the power you came here with. Success comes from within and with knowing that *you are the divine.*

In the chapters that follow, you will start to increase your vibration and frequency. Miracles will unfold naturally.

You are loved, you are worthy, you are capable of creating whatever you want in this lifetime.

This is something that you can read out loud to yourself as much or as little as you're called to support you with remembering your truth and inner wisdom:

Your Truth Will Set You Free

There are ancient truths in the soles of your feet. As you connect to Mother Earth.

To lead, so others can rise up with you.

You're a trailblazer.

A magical being.

You being in your energy, fully expressed, unapologetically you is more than enough.

You were created a miracle. This isn't big headed or too big for your britches — this is your truth.

I surrender to my TRUTH, I will stop fighting my MAGIC.

I am a visionary.

I am a conduit of light.

I am TRUTH.

And as I rise, as I surrender, I give others permission to do the same.

We are told to "just do it" or "just get on with it".

And we wonder why unhappiness breeds and lives in every crevice.

What if you aligned with source energy?

What if you created from true alignment?

What if our hearts opened?

What if we loved and enjoyed all of life's magic?

What if any intention you set came with ease and flow?

What if sacrifice was a thing of the past?

What if fun, play and pleasure was your natural way of being?

Would they stare?

Would they wonder how you receive so much joy?

Well, give them a reason to stare, to look your way.

Because when you dull down — you dull those looking to you for light.

You being all of you is all that is ever needed.

Whatever you desire, dear child. Is YOURS. Ask and you WILL receive.

All that I ever ask of you in this lifetime is to be YOU. YOU. YOU. YOU.

And then what would become of the old me?

She's given you what you needed. She has blessed you with the truth. But she is no longer you. Say Goodbye. Thank her dearly. Because she made you who you are.

But life is allowed to get better and better. How good will you let it get?

Life is a GIFT. It is FUN. You are here to be a visionary. To blaze a trail. To guide. To show. Not to cower to an old system.

Lead, Rise, Love, Hold, Feel, Surrender.

You are blessed, always.

I love you, you are resilient, you're worthy and you can create anything you want.

xox

Claim Back Your Power From Within

Hi, I'm Kylie Nel. Human Design Business coach, 4/6 Manifesting Generator, wife, wine-lover, fur mom—so many things all in one. My mission is to help female entrepreneurs (specifically coaches) build a 6-figure business legacy by activating their power from within, speaking their truth, and tailoring business strategies to be filled with pleasure, passion and profits. My work includes human design, quantum energy healing, leadership development, mindset and business strategy.

As I write this, I'm celebrating with my cold brew, soaking in a morning of spending time with my new horse, and feeling absolutely fucking in love with life and my business. But, it wasn't always this way.

I started working with Vanessa in December 2020, after experiencing my first 6-figure USD year. I was burnt out, anxious, and to be honest, miserable. So much felt unaligned... from the experiences I had with clients, to feeling disconnected to my vision, and truthfully just not being sure how I would continue to build a dream business, since it had turned into a nightmare.

The trauma I had experienced within my first 6-figure year stopped me from believing that I could be *paid to be me*. I had terrible experiences where clients bullied me, dropping out of my programs, and my identity had become so submerged within my business—I worked non-stop. I felt like my team no longer aligned with my vision, which resulted in loneliness and doubt in my discernment. I had gained weight, felt scared to continue, and questioned my path in the online space. There were so many mixed emotions of anger, resentment, shame, guilt, and deep sadness.

After doing an intensive with Vanessa (which changed my fucking life!), and then joining *Supercharge your Success by Design*, I had no idea what I was letting myself into. I've worked with a number of business coaches, invested well over $50K, and Vanessa just hit me at my core. The love I have for this woman and how she has changed my life is indescribable.

There were so many layers we had to work through, from mother wounding (which I never knew dominated and controlled how I showed up in my business to the extent it did), to reframing limiting beliefs and fears I had around success. To claim back my power and confidence from within. The concept of clients loving me for me, success coming with ease, and manifesting my desires (in business and life) to be second nature was foreign to me. I will never forget the messages from Vanessa: "You're doing it again..." as she called me out on my self-sabotaging cycle. Every time we'd hit a big breakthrough, I'd start all over again.

About five months later, everything started to shift, and I finally felt ready. I experienced one of the most profitable cash weeks in my business (working less than I ever have before), my investments for all my programs have gone up, I no longer obsess over business, I manifested a dream horse, and my husband and I have an incredible relationship with phenomenal sex.

Know that, once you start working with Vanessa you're not just in her vortex for business strategy (trust me, the strategy is there and she makes things so easy), but she is going to activate every single cell inside your being. Your personal relationships change, your perception of life changes, the way you live life changes. I have goosebumps writing this and tears in my eyes, because the shifts are radical.

Vanessa, I appreciate you more than a girl appreciates her red wine.

May you continue to impact millions, and make millions.

KYLIE NEL
kylienelcoaching.com

chapter 2

Having It All

I am a failure. How did I allow myself to get here?

There I was, crying for four hours in the bath. Huddled over, holding my knees and bowing my head in shame.

In May 2015, I was broken (and broke) after almost three months of trying to build the business full-time. I had blown through $15,000 in savings, had $400 left to my name, and I was unemployed. I was showing up online every day with new content, I had a website and professional photos, but only a couple of clients. And to add to it, they were only paying me $25/hour.

I was writing out affirmations such as: *I will get three clients at $1,500 before X date,* but my subconscious mind was telling me that that wasn't possible for me.

The reality is: it's never about just doing things. It's about the energy and belief behind it. When the doing is an extension of your most expressed self—that's where the magic happens.

The thought of returning to a corporate job was looking more and more like my reality.

Why can't I make this work? What is wrong with me? What am I missing?

A memory from my childhood surfaced. It was a beautiful summer day, and I was sitting on the steps outside the art studio at school in my favourite bell bottom high-waisted jeans and a pink spaghetti strap top. My best friend at the time, Taz, turned to me and said, "Vanessa, you're going to be super successful. I can see it."

I was 16 at the time, and I remember it like yesterday. This had given me unwavering faith that I would be a success. And yet, there I was, doubting everything and terrified that it was all a big, fat lie.

I started to believe that maybe all there was to life was to work hard, make enough money to pay the bills, and retire at 70.

As I continued to cry, my body heaved with deep anger, disappointment and sadness. I started to resign myself to an ordinary life. A life society tells us is *success*. Perhaps I was being unrealistic. How could a small-town girl like me possibly do what these other "prettier," "thinner," "smarter," and "more successful" women were doing?

Between the tears, I started searching for courses, programs and mentors. In the midst of all this, I signed up for a $497 course called *6 Weeks To $6K*. I thought I had done it all wrong. At this stage, having a $6K month and replacing my previous corporate salary felt out of reach. All I wanted to do was quit my corporate job, create a business on my terms, and replace my income.

The voice in my head grew louder saying: "You can't do this!"

All the while, my soul was screaming: "You are made for more! You are meant to create this!"

A knock on the door jolted me from this deep sadness. Shaun was home from work. I dragged myself out of the bath and cried in his arms, naked, lifeless and afraid. As he held me, he reassured me that I wasn't a failure. "If others can do it, so can you," he said. There was a glimmer of hope and a lightbulb moment.

You've achieved so much already in your life you can do this. You won't know how or when, but it's time to do whatever it takes to create a new reality.

This was a turning point for me. A dark moment with a powerful gift. It was at this point I knew I had to make this business work so that I could get out of my corporate job. I couldn't wake up 10 years from now wishing or hoping that I had created the freedom and flexibility I knew was meant for me—a life beyond the corporate cubicle.

I knew, like you, that I was born for incredible things. I spent many years doubting my magic and dimming my light. The same questions kept me up, night after night:

What if there isn't more to life? What if I'm not made for more?

I had a constant fixation on the next thing. I was always wondering *when life was going to begin*. Life became a perpetual cycle of being obsessed with the future, impatient to achieve goals, and being stuck in the past.

There is so much power and beauty in being in the present. The only thing that is truly real is this present moment.

PAID TO BE YOU MANTRA

Take a few deep belly breaths. Close your eyes. Settle into this incredible moment you have right now of being you—a divine and amazing being. Let your breath slow down as you connect to your core. The space where you are in flow. Listen to the heartbeat of mother nature. We are all one, together on this journey.

Abundance is my birthright, miracles are my birthright and magic is my birthright

I am wild

I am loved

I am more than enough

I am free

I joyfully release the past and expect the best now and in the future

THE BREAKDOWN BEFORE THE BREAKTHROUGH

The breakthrough often feels like it comes after a breakdown. In reality, the contraction is happening simultaneously with the expansion as we are being shaped for our next level of growth. It isn't either or.

How would growth happen if it was always easy-breezy? How would we know what true joy is if we haven't seen the opposite? How would we experience love if we haven't had fear (the opposite of love)?

It often takes people hitting rock bottom or getting ill to make a change. If you keep ignoring the signs, you will be pushed (or rather, shoved) back on to your authentic path. As a client once said: "First you get the feather, then comes the brick, and then the truck!"

You are being given signs all the time, it is important to slow down enough to pay attention, listen and take action in alignment with your intuition.

So often, we try to stay busy to avoid our truth. To avoid the pain. To avoid feeling. But, you're being invited to stop and listen.

When you clear the noise and come back to your truth, you actually find your magnifice, inner power, and who you really are.

Soul Reflection

Take a moment, a deep breath, and tap into your higher self. Consider the following questions:

- **What is that voice within me telling me right now?**
- **If I had $5 million dollars in my bank account, what would I do differently in my life and business?**
- **What feels exciting and exhilarating? What makes my body feel alive? What makes me feel every cell of my body activating? How does that feel?**

It's not easy, but sitting with this voice is key to *your* success. Radical honesty with yourself and others will set you free.

Your natural state is feeling vibrant, happy and living in flow. When I first awakened to my truth, it felt as if a million switches had been flipped on. I was buzzing with joy and enthusiasm. I was feeling everything so deeply and profoundly, from hearing a bird chirp, to enjoying food, to having sex, to showing up for live trainings, and getting messages from clients.

Coming alive, at first, is overwhelming and unfamiliar. It is why I fought it for many years (and why you might be fighting it right now). But illness, resistance, anxiety and feeling like everything is a struggle is *not* the way you're meant to feel. (Pushing bad feelings away is not the goal—we will discuss feeling all of the emotions in later chapters.) When we are in flow with divine source energy, wellbeing and abundance comes naturally in all areas of your life. You have the whole Universe moving through you. You are the divine.

When we ignore the signs, illness is a much needed wake-up call telling us that we need to align. However, most people just shove down a pill thinking that is the answer.

You will receive the wake up call, but your truth already resides within you. It's time to listen and be guided. To be quiet and to hear the whispers of your heart and soul. You have a purpose, a soul's calling, and a destiny. You are here for a reason.

The key is to recognise that if something feels off, if you have a multitude of destructive patterns (overspending, overeating, overworking, drama), if you lack joy in your life, or are plagued by not feeling good enough...it is time to go deeper, to connect to yourself, and to understand the shadow self while you show up with the next aligned action.

EVERYTHING IS HAPPENING FOR YOU, NOT TO YOU

Learning and truly understanding that everything is happening *for* me (and not *to* me) has been monumental in my healing and growth. In my life, the darkest moments brought the greatest gifts and for that, I am grateful. In spiritual psychology, it is believed that we choose our path, the lessons we are meant to learn, and that we even choose our parents and family.

Everything and everyone is a mirror for our growth and expansion. Our reality is simply a reflection of our internal world. You create your own reality—by changing your thoughts, words and actions, you can create incredible change in your life!

Things won't always work as your ego wants them to. A launch that doesn't go according to plan, clients that fall out of programs, and even your own self-sabotage, are all guiding you back to your core. It is all happening for your growth and evolution.

Some days you'll want to throw in the towel, give up, or go live in an Ashram. Those days are key defining moments allowing you to reconnect deeply to *why* you're doing what you do.

Some clients come into your world to trigger you to change, others will show you your shadow self, and others will come back year after year for their next evolution. I've worked with some clients four times over six years! Everything is happening cyclically and we always get what we need to grow, but it takes paying attention and observing yourself to truly expand.

The only thing that is truly real, is what we *think is real.* Read that again.

Soul Reflection

Think about your life right now. Pull back and see it from a wider perspective. Is there something specific happening in your life that is difficult, but could turn into an opportunity for growth? Answer the following questions:

- What is the lesson I need to learn from this experience?
- Why is this happening for my growth and evolution?
- If I learned the lesson, what would I now put in place/shift?

THE TURNING POINT

I made the decision to take out a business loan to hire a business coach. I don't believe that everyone needs a business coach, but for me, investing in myself in that way was the aligned move. I decided to believe fully in making it work, no matter what. I was showing up for myself saying: "I am worth it." Being brave enough to ask for support shifts a lot.

You don't have to try and do this all alone.
In fact, doing it together is far more fun!

Having skin in the game and accountability compresses your timeline. No one can save or fix you—you have to be ready for change and committed to the discomfort that change brings.

I set a clear date to leave my corporate job. Although I didn't know how I was going to do it, I knew that I was meant to have my own business and create a ripple effect of change in the world.

Working with women and helping them transform their lives made me come alive with joy. It lit me up. It gave me purpose

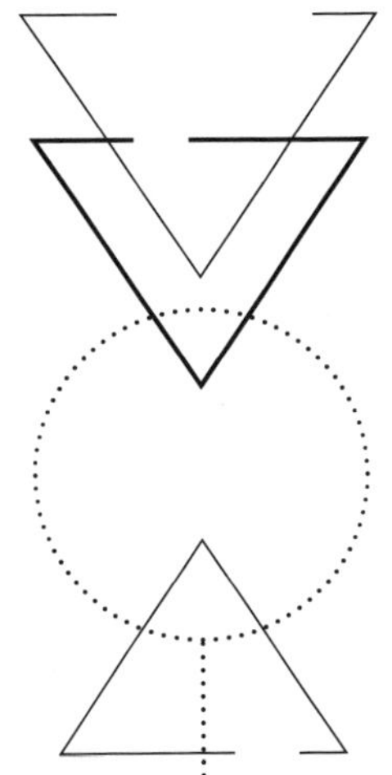

You don't have to try and do this all alone. In fact, doing it together is far more fun!

and fulfillment. But the journey to being paid to be me has been a wild ride of highs, lows and an emotional rollercoaster. It was a rollercoaster that I wouldn't change for anything, but I wish this book existed to help *me.*

Building your business is the greatest personal development journey. When we start out, most people think that it is all about the website, branding, getting clients, navigating marketing and creating programs. We think that we need to hustle, work long hours, and do tons of things we don't like. But we soon get to realise that true success and having it all is a deep journey into understanding and knowing yourself so intimately that you *know* that there is no competition. That you are the only choice for your soul clients, crucial to their particular journey, and that marketing can be fun when it is done in an aligned way (more on this later).

When you set a powerful intention, understand your limiting beliefs and habits, and take the aligned action with absolute faith, incredible things unfold. Magic, abundance and miracles are your birthright. Having it all is your birthright. Making money and creating a life beyond your wildest imagination can (and will) come with ease and flow.

We are taught that ambition and success comes with sacrifice—with a constant fear of waiting for one shoe to drop. The truth is, we don't have to sacrifice one area of our life for success, but we do need to put energy into dialling up *all* areas of our lives to a high standard.

Although it sounds backwards, many clients tell me they have a fear of success. I believe the fear of success is really a fear of the unfamiliar. This is completely normal, as the brain likes the familiar and will take the path of least resistance. So, in order to manifest and create a new reality, we need to create familiarity with what you actually want, and create a clear picture of what success looks like for *you.* If you're envisioning someone else's version of success, *of course* it is scary. But your version of success that is created from alignment and truth, is invigorating!

But even when we plan exactly what we want, know that we will constantly be surprised with even better.

Steps To Having It All:

1. Identify what *having it all* really means to you. My version of success will be totally different from yours. Start to define it for yourself. Listen deeply into the niggle deep inside; what your soul is guiding you to, and what you've been ignoring. Be unapologetic about your desires in your relationship, business, life and health.
2. Believing you get to have it all, releasing any limiting beliefs, and giving yourself permission to listen to your soul desires is key to having it all.
3. Make sure it is safe to have what you want. If what you want hasn't shown up, on some level it may not be safe. It may benefit you more subconsciously to stay where you are or your nervous system may not be ready to take on more. Recognise and own this so that you can unlock what is truly holding you back.
4. Show up and take the aligned action like the version of you that already has it all. We can't expect a different outcome if we show up in our current identity.

▷ If what I want is already taken care of,
how would I show up now?

▷ If what I want is already taken care of, what would I create?

We will go through these steps in the chapters to come, as you start to truly embrace that you get to have it all on your terms, without sacrificing your health, happiness and relationships.

RELEASING THE CURSED *HOW*

Want an incredible business, relationship and body? Ask yourself: *if I already had an amazing business, body, conscious relationship, and tons of money...what would my thoughts, words, energy and actions of this version of me look like? What does that version of me really want and need?*

Your body has incredible wisdom. It knows how it wants to move, it knows what will fuel it for optimal health, and it knows how it wants to be loved. I learned this on my journey as I healed my relationship with my body. After years of hating my body, binge eating, and obsessively weighing myself, the one question that changed everything was: *Vanessa, what do you need right now?* I have used this question in every area of my life, and it has profoundly changed my path for the better. I urge you to stop and do the same to start tuning in and reconnecting to your body. It can be trusted. You can trust yourself.

We so often overcomplicate things, trying to find something outside of ourselves to fix, save or change us. I truly believe everything you need to create a wildly successful business and life is already within you.

Everything you need is already within you, right now, if you slow down to listen.

There is no point being fixated on the outcome, as most of us have this wrong. I certainly did! If you keep asking *how* you'll hit 7-figures, and make decisions based on that, you'll get fixated on the outcome. You should definitely still play with possibility and have fun with dreaming and being at that frequency, but overly obsessing or doing things just to hit a specific goal will be exhausting and a recipe for burnout.

If you follow this approach, you'll often end up selling what you think you should sell and make business decisions based on what others do, instead of truly listening in to what you're guided to do.

When you show up with passion and purpose, and embody the energy of the version of you that already has exactly as you desire, there is a powerful shift in energy.

You are an original. No one is you and that is your superpower. The more you embrace who you are and follow what you are guided to create, the more life will flow. The Universe is always conspiring for you.

Your next level is not in doing more. It's not about a number either. It's about cultivating boundaries, emotional intelligence, honouring yourself, balancing your energy and speaking your truth. It is about setting yourself free. Knowing that everything you desire is already taken care of.

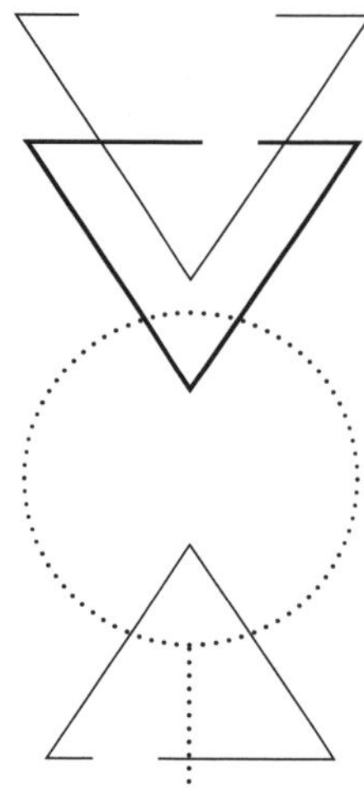

Everything you need is already within you, right now, if you slow down to listen.

Soul Reflection

- What would feel incredibly expansive in my schedule, and in what I sell? (Set your schedule up in this way and sell what you desire now.)
- How would I show up in my business if it was already done? How would I dress? What activities am I called to do? (Show up in that way now.)

Close your eyes. Visualise the version of you that has exactly what you desire, making the impact and income that is meant for you with ease. Embody how you feel, activate the confidence and the decisions you're making.

- What would happen if I showed up like everything I desire is already done with complete certainty? (If you want to write a book, write a page a day or set up time in your schedule where it is non-negotiable. If you want consistent income and clients in your business, set your business up for consistency. You can't expect consistency if you haven't created a pathway for consistency.)
- If I had consistent months in my business I would...
- Where am I not being consistent?
- If I want consistency what does my business model look like?

If you've created your version of success in one area of your life, you can do it in others. How you do one thing is how you do everything.

Leave space for magic! It gets even better than you could ever imagine. Miracles are happening in every moment when we allow ourselves to see them.

Remember the results and income you receive are not in direct relation to how much you do, it is the energy that you do it in.

LEAP AND THE NET WILL APPEAR

I was Little Ness with bunches in her hair, quietly confident but petrified of speaking in class because of fear of being judged or looking stupid.

This book is a reminder that life can change in miraculous ways, and your past does not define your future.

I have transformed from being quietly confident and afraid of speaking in class to selling millions of dollars of programs online, being visible, and impacting thousands of lives. I've done this while living my dream life with my fiancé, Shaun, and golden retriever, Apollo. This has taken a lot of mindset, heartset, marketing, and energy work. It has taken investments when it felt incredibly scary, following my intuition, and leaping even when I don't know if the net will appear.

We have to learn to leap and allow the net to appear. We can't expect the net to be there before we leap.

Each time you take a step outside of your comfort zone and follow through on something you're being guided to do, your faith in yourself increases until doing bigger things becomes even easier.

Take a moment to consider:

- ▷ With the change that you want to make right now in your business, what would faith do?
- ▷ If you fully trusted yourself and absolutely knew without a doubt that you were guided and supported, what would you do differently?

I have 100% faith that I get to have it all, and so do you. You get to have an incredible life, an amazing relationship, lots of money, a profound impact on others, and an overflow of love and wealth to give freely.

***The more you see money as good,
the more you amplify the good in the world.***

You get to sell the program you really want, share the message that is coming through you, attract soul clients, and make as much money as you want.

As I always say to my clients: *it is done*. Because it is. That version of you already exists in the quantum realm.

You get to decide. But first: make the darn decision.

If you're ready (and I know you are), say this mantra out loud:

I decide, I am ready to have it all on my terms without sacrifice. Whatever I want is already on its way to me.

When you say yes to your soul, your soul says yes to you.

Life is either a daring adventure or a series of what if's. What if today you consciously created your dream life and business?

Having It All Using Your Gifts

The burning desire to be more, do more, and to contribute more to the world had always been in the back of my head....but how was I supposed to do that failing school, being perfectly average, and feeling like I was too dumb to achieve the reach that I wanted to? Not to mention the fact that I had no idea what my message was.

I just knew I wanted to help people.

I was a hairdresser for 20 years and I absolutely loved it. I was fantastic at hearing what others required and giving advice.

After my second child was born, I hit burnout. I had the side hustle working from my home salon and two children that didn't sleep. I couldn't keep up with everyone else! I drank alcohol to relax and coffee to stay awake. I was a secret hot mess.

My exhaustion and depression became so bad that I couldn't leave bed unless I was to go to work or had to tend to the children.

On the outside I looked happy, but on the inside I felt like I was slowly dying, and that fire I once had for living was fading out. *Was this life?*

I knew I was intuitive and had psychic abilities—it ran in my family—but with my Catholic upbringing, I wasn't sure about what was right or wrong. I was taught not to tap into those abilities and not to share them with the world.

Tarot cards and talking about spirit communication was *dabbling* and not tolerated! I was told to give them up to God, not speak about them, and pray for those 'new age' people.

This never felt right to me, but I wanted to be a *good girl.* Being the eldest of five, I was exceptional at being the good girl and the ultimate people-pleaser.

Naturally, I was a brilliant hard worker who did not like to go against the rules, so going against the grain wasn't ideal. On the other hand, my natural creativity, my different ways of viewing the world, and my extreme psychic powers were creating inner conflict. My psychic gifts started to become stronger. I felt more connected to spirit than I was with humans, which was becoming a serious problem.

I had to make a choice to conform, or to break through and choose to be more conscious. At the time, I had no idea what I was doing, but intuitively I knew that my fire was going to go out if I didn't make a choice.

I had faith in myself and made a bold decision.

I chose to live and committed to myself to never go back to where I'd been. To choose what I believed in, and to find my purpose here on Earth, so I could share my message with the world and let other women know they can choose who they truly are. They could also be happy and have it all! BOLD AF!

Despite knowing I was a psychic medium, I hadn't done readings yet, so I wasn't sure what my message was. I hired my first coach to help, which was my first big step towards shifting. Over the next few years, I managed to create a business as a Spiritual Empowerment Coach.

I have created digital programs, one-on-one clients, and created a platform including podcasts, social media, and even created a summit called "Mom's Time to Shine," where I've helped thousands of people by sharing tools, processes and mindset shifts. (It's important to note that all of this was still possible to me, despite how *not* techy I am!)

When I stepped into the shadows of my fear and turned up the gratitude, I was able to see my path and message clearly. Suddenly, I knew what my superpowers were.

Now this is a message I share with others!

Believing that I could be paid just to be me was the next level. When Vanessa invited me to this way of thinking, it took me a little while to get my head around it. It's not normal in this reality!

I was taught that money sold programs. One of my programs was based on money and how you could use your gifts to make money. I sold my programs by telling people they could make money too, but I was hiding *my true gifts* and attracting non-ideal clients.

Here's what I learned...

- The truth of following the energy on who I desire to work with.
- The truth of manifesting the money by aligning to your design.
- The truth of being in true joy when offering your programs.
- The truth of following my heart and leading with my heart, not scarcity.

(These were way more aligned in my sales calls than using money as my sales strategy.)

When I started working with Vanessa, I asked her specifically to show me structures and systems, so I could expand my reach and make more money.

Here's how I understood success: the more people I reached and the more money I made, the more successful I would be. This was my limited point of view.

Vanessa showed me that I still required mindset, energy shifting, and soul alignment to really hit those big numbers and to fulfill my dreams of getting my message out and to reach the goals I desired. What I learned was that it wasn't about how many clients, systems in place, or how many sales calls I had. It was about coming home to who I am, being in my own divine energy, and letting the ripple effect come from that place.

Human Design was a big part of this that changed my life when I realised I can make money by being *me*. In fact, going for a walk on the beach will make me a lot more money than sitting in front of the computer. **This was next level!**

Having Vanessa as a coach opened my mind to more possibilities. I managed to triple the amount of money that was coming in very quickly from $10K months to $30K months. I even had a $60K month. Ironically, in the $60K month, I did no more work and I actually went to the beach more. People were drawn in because of my energy.

My husband quit his job and is working full time in our business, we built a house and I realised my best program yet was all about mediumship. I also use my conscious coaching, light language, and energy healing in all I do.

With Vanessa, I was able to:

- Drop all the judgments of the religion, and what is right and the wrong.
- Drop all the judgments of what I thought other people thought of me.
- Drop the judgments of how I'm supposed to work.
- Drop the judgments of how my worthiness is meant to come to me.
- Drop the people pleasing.
- Drop the hustle mode.
- Drop the emergency.
- Drop drama patterns, and the obsession with reaching goals.

Vanessa could see the things that I didn't see, the unconscious patterns, and help me transmute them before my very eyes!

I wouldn't believe that I can be paid to be me without seeing it. Vanessa showed me the *how.*

We all hear of coaches saying these things, but it seems too good to be true, so we either don't try or we try too hard. I knew I had the tendency to do the latter, so I took a step back and chose to trust and have faith.

What I did was I trusted and I had faith.

Faith in my beautiful coach Vanessa.

Faith in myself.

Faith in the Universe, that it was going to work, and that I would take aligned action when required.

Knowing that Spirit was here to guide me and all of those around me would love me anyway, no matter what I chose.

Because choosing *me* was the biggest thing that would transform all of those around me.

Supercharge Your Success By Design is a next-level program. This is something where I'm allowed to come out and transform myself and be held in a space of love, gratitude and support.

This is a place where I am the CEO and the queen of my own empire, and where I shift my soul energy to get rid of another layer, every time to expand and evolve with ease.

This is where I take a Quantum Leap and have all of my dreams come true, faster than ever before.

I'm so grateful that I followed my gut (and not my head) by choosing the right coach at the right time!

Now I'm purely paid to be me.

Vanessa is more than a coach. She is a soul-shifter!

VICTORIA BOND, Spiritual Success Coach
www.victoriabond.co.nz

chapter 3

Creating Success On Your Terms

We are all born with a blueprint of success that is unique to our soul lessons and curriculum. I use a variety of modalities including Human Design and Gene Keys to help my clients embody their authentic gifts. The purpose and gifts that each person uniquely has. My gifts are: authenticity and helping others step into their truth, teaching others to create financial abundance, I'm a natural saleswoman, and I'm here to help others with self love. A lot of my soul lessons thus far have been centred around getting myself to a space of knowing who I am and loving myself.

- What do you love to speak about?
- What do clients come to you for most?
- What sets your soul on fire?

In spiritual psychology, soul agreements are contracts made between two or more individuals before they enter this physical realm. Souls choose relationships and family ties based on lessons they wish to learn in human form. We choose our lessons. It is also why our soul clients are already meant to work with us and are in your vortex—and why worrying, not listening to our intuition, and not honouring the lessons we are meant to learn (and patterns we are meant to break) may stop the flow.

My definition of success is going to be different than yours. When you release and surrender to a force greater than you, knowing that you are always guided and protected, you can allow true magic, miracles and inner peace to come into your life. It doesn't mean that you can't choose what you want and make decisions— you *do* have free will. You are not controlled by something external. In fact, the divine/god/source *is* you. We are all one. There is no separation.

You being in your purpose, sharing your unique gifts, and owning just how brilliant you are, will shift the paradigm.

You are a genius.

You are magnificent.

There is nothing to prove.

Simply, be more of your authentic self. The more you are you, the more money you make. The more you are you, the more magnetic you become.

Uncovering and understanding what is true for *you* and what success is for *you,* is crucial to living a limitless life and receiving divine compensation for your unique gifts.

Remember: you don't have to do, have, or create *anything* to be successful. Being born means you are a success. You are a miracle. You have the power of the Universe within you. You have a purpose and reason for being here and when you align fully with this, whatever is meant for you will drop in. Whatever is meant for you is already in your personal energetic field and to be able to fully receive this, we need to learn the lessons, and let go of self limiting beliefs. Within your energy field, you are surrounded by limitless potential.

I am successful now.

It doesn't mean that things will always go the way our ego wants—in fact, this is where true growth happens. You'll get infinitely better at managing whatever happens and seeing it is a way to evolve.

I often look at life like a cosmic game. Master your inner world, understand your gifts, remember your brilliance, and own you are worthy and unique. That is the next level.

YOUR SUCCESS BLUEPRINT

I was brought up to believe that success was making loads of money, having a big house, being an accountant or lawyer, and driving a Mercedes Benz. My dad was an accountant but started farming when he moved to Knysna. He drove an old Mercedes that he seemed to be always fixing. We lived in a very old farmhouse. The water we bathed in was often dark from mud—the cows would often go into the dam where the water was pumped from. I received hand-me-downs from my older sister, Jenée. We weren't able to afford fashionable and expensive items like some of the other kids at school.

It was deeply ingrained into my mind that "money doesn't grow on trees" and "it takes hard work to make money." Perhaps you can relate?

I know that my dad wanted a different life for us. One where we didn't struggle financially and where we had a secure job. We were taught that keeping up appearances and showing the outside world that everything was fine and dandy was a way of life.

In my business, trying to keep up appearances and show the outside world that I had it all together played out in different ways. I would wake up at 3:00 a.m. in a panic and answer messages from clients while on the toilet. I didn't want to let anyone down. I didn't want to disappoint anyone. Most importantly, I didn't want to be seen as lazy. I was so afraid of losing it all and having to admit to the outside world that I didn't have it all together.

The anxiety mounted as I took on too much responsibility for clients and lacked boundaries. The cracks were starting to appear.

Although my childhood was filled with playing tennis on the lawn, outdoor adventures, running down to the dam to swim, and the bliss of farm life, it was also filled with financial highs and lows. One Christmas we would have gifts, a beautiful dinner and the next, the cars were broken down, we had no money to fix them, and we walked to the local restaurant for a plate of fries.

One weekend, I remember driving back from a friend's house, wondering whether there would be food on the table when I got home. At the final hour, my dad would sell something on the farm. Amidst this uncertainty, I always believed that "money was there when we needed it" but I thought that money only came from hardship, struggle and hitting a low point.

From an early age I adopted the belief that success was something external to me. Success was in acquiring material things and having more stuff.

Ironically, I now drive a Mercedes, live in a beautiful five-bedroom home, and make an incredible amount of money running my own business. Fortunately, I feel like I retired at 34. Every day, I get to do my soul's work and fill my days with *so much* pleasure and joy. I believe that when you do the work you're meant to, it doesn't feel like work. I am in constant awe and gratitude that I get paid to write, speak, create, learn and transform lives.

It wasn't always this way. With all the striving, pushing and proving, no matter what I acquired, I never felt like it was enough.

I was terrified of everything I'd built crumbling. I was always worried about losing it all. It kept me up at night. No matter how much money I made, I worried about not making enough. I would also feel extreme guilt making money in my business and would argue with Shaun when we spent too much. I could never seem to enjoy it. I remember one day, in the midst of launching a program with sales pouring in, Shaun and I were at a top Michelin-star restaurant in the glitzy centre of Singapore. We had booked a gorgeous room in the Marina Bay Sands Hotel that had an infinity pool on the 57th floor overlooking the city. The bill arrived for the delicious meal, and I picked a fight with Shaun.

"We are so wasteful, how could we have spent so much? This is ridiculous," were the words that came out of my mouth.

This was a big moment for me. I gained a lot of awareness in that experience about how I always ruined things that were fun.

My heart still sinks thinking about being in that state around money. We had the money and wanted to have a gorgeous dinner. This outburst, I later realised, was one of many occasions I ruined. I didn't know how to have fun. This was a learned behaviour. My dad would ruin every occasion that was special and unconsciously I repeated this. This wasn't his fault, as he learned it too, but it's our responsibility now to heal these wounds. Having too much fun can feel unfamiliar and like losing control when life has been filled with a lot of pain and struggle.

It was also aligned with the beliefs that were instilled in me around money, such as: "rich people have more money than sense," and "making money is hard." I had a lot of guilt and shame around spending money because of my conditioning.

Our launch generated over $137,000 and we had 6-figures in savings. The dinner was expensive for what we were used to, but it was something we wanted to do. There is something really beautiful about going to a Michelin star restaurant, not looking at the price, and ordering exactly as you want. Let's stop ruining magical moments that are meant to be savoured!

After a heated argument, going to bed angry, and deep disappointment at how many times I ruined moments in my life like this, I vowed that this would be the last. If I made the decision to eat out and spend money on something I desired, I would savour, enjoy and relish in the moment. And then, I would turn that pleasure up.

In these moments, instead of fearing the unfamiliar feeling of having fun and trying to automatically ruin it to go back to the familiar, I say: "This is good, this feels different, it's safe, and if I was to feel even better, what would that look like?"

Remember, life is allowed to get better and better. How good will you let it get?

Are you ready to dismantle the beliefs you have about money? Are you truly ready to feel the splendour and joy of this human experience?

I used to believe that spending money investing in myself or learning was good, and spending money on Louis Vuitton bags, first-class flights, and expensive dinners was bad. This isn't true— it is only good or bad if you make it so. When you honour your soul desires, you expand your vibration and frequency, which expands your energetic capacity to receive.

If you are filled with guilt, overworking, selling programs you hate and are exhausted, how would that ever lead to receiving more?

When life was too good, it felt like I was losing control and would pick a fight or ruin a moment to come back to the familiar feeling of pain and struggle. Our brains will choose the path of least resistance, perpetuating old habits and patterns, unless we change them.

It was exhausting being in a constant state of fear and never feeling good enough.

Newsflash! You were born worthy, you are a miracle, and you are incredible at what you do. You've simply forgotten your magic and power.

It's time to awaken fully to your truth, your magic and to break the habits and patterns that keep you in the familiar.

THE FACADE OF SUCCESS

It's easy to be eluded by what "success" and "failure" is and isn't. Everyday we are bombarded online with the perfect Instagram life, expensive luxury lifestyle, and seeing others travel to exotic destinations. The "freedom-based business" and "laptop lifestyle" is portrayed in a fairytale way. There are talented people thinking that if they're not speaking about money or living this lifestyle, they can't possibly be successful. Entrepreneurs are trying to fit into a box, sell cookie-cutter programs, and copy messages from others. All the while, they are racking up credit card debt, buying fancy items out of their means, and taking selfies in first class to appear successful. To feel something. Behind the scenes it's a shit show.

I can say this confidently because this was *my* behind the scenes (minus the credit card debt). I thought that success was something external and that my lifestyle and how much money I made was why clients wanted to work with me. What I know now is that people buy into who I am, my energy, and the authenticity I bring.

There are particular clients that are meant to work with you in this lifetime and all you're required to do is be unapologetically you.

What if you could have the material things you desire while feeling amazing? What if making money came from you being authentically you, speaking your truth, and sharing your signature offers?

What if all the material things were absolutely taken care of and you never worried about them? What if you trusted it was already done?

What would it create space for you to focus on? How much more time and energy would you have to create if you had faith that you were always taken care of? (You are!)

Let's break up with sacrifice. Let's break up with the idea that it takes hard work to make money. Let's break up with the idea that if you're not exhausted or suffering in some way, you can't have what you want.

Let's remember that you were born worthy.

When you honour your soul desires, you expand and vibrate at a higher frequency. I love beautiful luxurious holidays and flying business class, but none of that determines my worth. None of that determines the success of my business. My business is a success because I was born a success, I was born with a soul purpose and a unique blueprint, and I follow through on what I am guided to do and create. Your business will be a success because you were born a success.

But we can still normalise wealth, luxury and playing with what we truly desire.

There is another way to create business. One of truth, alignment and inner peace. But to create what you're meant to, the old way, beliefs and identity need to be shed. There needs to be a dismantling of who you think you are, to be who you're meant to be.

YOUR WEALTH BLUEPRINT IS WITHIN

When you create wealth from within, use your unique gifts in the way that you're meant to, and create programs that only you can, you don't fear losing your business or not making enough money. You have faith that you are infinitely abundant and guided.

I know this intimately because I was caught up in the whirlwind of trying to look successful to the outside world and following what that version of success was. I was living my dream life in Bali with everything I *thought* I wanted, and yet, I was miserable. I was filled with anxiety and constantly worrying about clients leaving, not getting results, failed payments, and taking on way too much responsibility. Looking back, the scariest and saddest part was that I had convinced myself that I *was* happy. After all, I had the vision board life...how could I not be happy?

Sadly, (but fortunately) it took burning out and hitting my rock bottom to find true happiness and contentment. It took wanting to end my life to realise that I had placed most of my worthiness on what I acquired. I thought that the only way out of the embarrassment, fear of being seen as a failure, and losing the business was to end my life. I genuinely believed that it wasn't worth living if I didn't have those things. That is deeply sad. Fortunately, wanting to end my life *gave me life.* It gave me a new way of being, a new appreciation for life, and a new presence in the gift of being on this planet at this time in history.

In fact, the less exhausted and the less you sacrifice yourself, the more money and clients you truly can attract. That success, happiness and love is not something you need to seek outside of you. It's something that is and always will be within you.

I know what it feels like to be caught up in a paradigm of working harder, doing more, and needing more results. To be constantly feeling like you're not good enough. I've been there— being fixated on getting the next client and the next payment to feel worthy. Although these things should be celebrated, the addiction and rush is fleeting and short-lived. Your emotions are at the effect of something external, and *oh boy,* is it a roller coaster to ride the highs and lows of each "hit".

There is a better way. Let me show you.

UNDERSTANDING YOUR OUTDATED PROGRAMMING

Most of what you believe today is outdated programming based on the first eight years of your life. We move through life following someone else's version of success because of beliefs that were instilled in us growing up.

When you are born, you have no logic, reason or inhibitory processes. To make your needs known you use primitive mechanisms such as crying, screaming, and tantrums. Often these behaviours are not seen as acceptable, so we learn to be quiet. This is the beginning of programming ourselves to be seen and not heard, to take up less space in the world, and to not upset others. It is also where we start to perceive certain emotions as "good" or "bad," so we can block out the "bad" ones in order to receive the love and acceptance of our parents and guardians.

But, the more you shove down your rage, anger, and sadness, the more you feel disconnected from yourself. Those emotions don't have anywhere to go, and so they are channelled into unhealthy patterns.

Babies are born with two fears: loud noises, and falling. Everything else is therefore learned through identification and association. Even your fear of visibility, speaking your truth, and being seen in a big way. *I see you!*

From the time you were born to approximately eight years old, you develop a library of these identifications and associations. We learn that some things are good and some things are bad. These positive and negative associations become a life script. Before we have logical reasoning, we will blame ourselves for things that happen. Without understanding these associations, we go through life unconsciously and continue to operate from the past.

Are you ready to create a deeper conscious awareness?

Identifications lead to associations, which then lead to emotions. If you were bullied as a child and called names, you may end up making the association that all women are bullies. This may stop you from creating meaningful relationships later on in life with women, to distrust other women, and to see them as competition. It is important to create awareness around the sisterhood wound and healing how we see other women so that we can shift how we show up in the world. Now more than ever, we are coming together, rising up, and collectively supporting each other. If we don't trust other women or if we see them as a threat or separate from us, how can we effortlessly attract them into our businesses? How can we collectively rise up together?

We are very receptive during these formative years because our right brains are active and the left brain—which includes critical thinking—is not yet fully functional. It's during those formative years that programming of the subconscious mind naturally occurs. It's how people take on limiting beliefs that sabotage their success. We adopt limiting beliefs such as thinking we are *too much, too loud,* or *too confident.* We start to believe that being authentically ourselves is not enough, and that we have to change to be liked. However, most of these memories aren't a real account. It's often a distortion, generalisation, or deletion. It is why what you believe about what happened and how that impacts you now, is more important than the memory itself.

None of the fears you currently have around visibility, selling your programs, or launching something are real threats, but the subconscious has stored an incident that may be holding you back. Without being conscious of the belief and being able to observe the pattern, you continue to follow out the same actions in alignment with this stored incident.

WHEN DID YOU FORGET YOUR MAGNIFICENCE?

Most of my life I tried to play the role of the good girl. I was conditioned away from my wild ways. As women, we are so often discouraged from expressing ourselves fully. I'm sure you can relate.

We are made to think that if you're not the good girl, then you're the whore. That there is no in between. I so badly wanted approval and wanted everyone to like me. I genuinely believed that by getting good grades and excelling at school I would get there.

I vividly remember the moment I lost my spark. It was like night and day. One moment I recall playing, dancing and running down to the river where we lived. The memory is often embellished with me dancing around with a colourful scarf, carefree and happy, but that memory of joy fades quickly as it is replaced by this sense of darkness. I had to grow up quickly—my parents were not fully present because of my father's illness, and all of the fun seemed to be sucked from my life.

I learned at a young age that *fun* was not something that was allowed. That we had to start learning to fend for ourselves and take care of ourselves. That life was hard.

Around this time I started rebelling at school, my grades dropped, and I was kicked out of most classes. Our financial situation worsened as my father was unable to work and my mom was forced to leave her teaching job.

My spark was lost, my childhood play and innocence long gone, and all I was left with was anger, resentment and a life filled with being serious. Sadly, there are very few carefree moments in my childhood that I can recall. I even struggled to have fun in university. I remember one Friday night, other students were having a party next door. Instead of joining the fun, I marched next door and complained about the noise. This over-seriousness continued into my adult life, until I burned out in 2018 and was forced to reassess my life.

Soul Reflection

- When did I forget my magnificence?
- What parts of myself do I need to call back? (Maybe in those parts you lost your self expression, your fun, your joy. Name it.)

- ▷ What do I need to remember about myself as a child? What do I need to release from my childhood? (If you have a photo of yourself as a child, take out the one that resonates with you the most.)
- ▷ What do I need to say to that version of myself now?

Hand on heart, take a deep breath in…

I call back the lost soul fragments

I call back the parts of me that I have neglected to own

I call back the parts that I've forgotten

I forgive my journey

I honour the lessons

I am ready to release myself from the past

I am free to be me

Most of your magnetic content, gifts and programs are hidden in the trauma and what we disenfranchise from. Yes, your most potent money making gifts are often the very things you are hiding and are the most easy for you! Let's call them back and own them.

FEELING GOOD AND SUCCESS

Feeling good to me used to mean: achieving Instagram-worthy goals, being ready to go on Facebook Live at any moment, and having *so much energy* to do all the activities I could possibly do. Now, feeling good to me means: honouring my emotions without judging myself and following my inner guidance moment to moment. I try to avoid using the words "feeling good" altogether, so I can connect to the emotion I feel without attaching judgement or moral value (good or bad). I feel *sad,* I feel *happy,* I feel *excited, etc.* This starts to build emotional intelligence by naming and honouring how you really feel.

Before I burned out, I had a deep-rooted belief that I wasn't worthy of feeling vibrant, radiant and happy.

Earlier I mentioned that when I'd feel at ease, it would feel like I was losing control. I would then self-sabotage so that I could feel the familiar feeling. If I didn't have something to fix, I didn't know who I was. But today, I get to feel at peace *all the time* because I've redefined what feeling good means to me. I choose to feel it.

Your emotions are not defined by how much you do, how much money you make in a day, how much you nap, the results your clients get, or how much you show up online. When how you feel is dependent on something external, you'll always feel fear around losing it, because that external reason can be taken away.

Feeling good—for lack of a better term—and being connected to divine source energy is our natural state. Channeling our message, being connected to our intuition, and having a deep sense of knowing our power is our natural state. Worry and panic does not serve anything. It can feel familiar, but it is not inherently you. However, there are ways to process all of these feelings and work with it (we will get to that later).

The Universe wants you to feel joy, it wants to support you, and it wants to guide you toward exactly what is meant for you.

When we realign with our power and the energy of love, there is nothing external that can shift that. You are worthy of feeling good all the time. You are worthy of whatever you desire. When you accept your magnificence and connect back into the power you came here with, naturally, you will be paid to be you.

The questions I come back to on a daily basis are:

- ▷ What do I feel most excited, energised and aligned with creating today?
- ▷ How can I be of service in the world today for the highest good of humanity?
- ▷ If I truly honoured myself and did exactly as I wanted for myself what would I do, how would I spend my time?

REDEFINING SUCCESS WITHOUT SACRIFICE

It's time to start to question the beliefs you have and uncover your truth so that you can remember your own brilliance, purpose, and power in the world and consciously create your reality. When we connect back to the inner power we came here with (yes, power is absolutely necessary), whatever is meant for us can actually drop in without resistance.

Often being in your power can be viewed in a negative light. It certainly has a shadow side when an individual uses their power to manipulate or control others. It is often why when it is thrown around without context, it is easy to confuse our perceptions of it.

First off, let's define power for *you*. It's very likely that your perception of power may be different to mine. Being in my power for me is owning my truth, being unapologetically me, sharing my gifts with the world, and not being held back by anything external. It is about feeling inner peace, confidence, and an inner knowing that I am gifted and inherently worthy and loved exactly as I am. My inner power connects me to all that is and allows me to have deep faith in my inner wisdom and guidance. My power allows me to be all of me, without fear of judgement or being an outcast.

- ▷ What does being in your power mean to you? Think of the first definition that comes to mind.
- ▷ Are there negative connotations or associations that you have? (E.g. being too aggressive, being overly controlling.)
- ▷ How do you feel when you're in your power?

I loved what a client said about her power:

"Power is speaking my truth, sharing what I know, and boldly showing up online so others can be impacted by my message."

Using what you discovered in the questions above, write a definition of power for yourself. Once you've discovered your version of being in your power and *embodying* it, you can start to really uncover your unique success blueprint.

Soul Reflection

Let's explore and uncover more about your soulful success blueprint:

- ▷ What does success really look like for you? How does success feel?

- ▷ What have you been told success should look like?
- ▷ What habits do you have that sabotage your success?

  E.g. guilt, addiction to struggle/hard, overeating

- ▷ If you created your version of success and consciously created your reality, what are the new thoughts, words, energy, feelings and actions?
- ▷ What are the rules and regulations you've created for yourself?

  E.g. bed times, when to work, how to create content, the programs you should sell

- ▷ What rules need to be released?

SOULFUL GOALS

My first ever group program launch in 2015 was a $40K launch. Of course, for my first launch it was amazing in terms of money received, but it was exhausting, and I adopted the belief that launching was exhausting. Everywhere I looked online, people were saying the same thing (your brain will find any evidence to support what you're thinking). Since changing my belief and launching when I want and how I want, things have completely shifted. We've had multiple 6-figure launches with ease, fun and joy. Although I love big launches from time to time, my business also has evergreen enrollment for consistency, sustainability and reliable income (great for my root chakra for safety and security). With evergreen enrollment, clients can join throughout the year at any time. I have a sales funnel in place and information available on my website.

In that first launch, I followed all the shoulds, musts, and have-tos. I ended up doing a five-day challenge followed by a webinar. These were never ways that I had purchased in the past, so why would I do them in my business? Of course, being that it was not in alignment, it was filled with stress. No one bought after the webinar and after quite a few posts, I decided to change the program and get it aligned to what I *wanted* to sell.

I asked myself: *what are the thoughts, words, energy, and actions of the me that has 20+ new clients with ease?* I reminded myself that the right clients will always arrive in the right quantity, which allowed me to surrender. I let go, knowing that if I continued to show up, speak my truth, and be in service to my audience, soul clients would arrive exactly as they needed.

The only strategy you need is the one you truly believe in. It is never about how you sell, but the energy behind it. I've done all the things, the way I should do them and felt exhausted. Remember: You are the strategy.

I went from stressed-out to a sold-out launch. Over the years, I have refined this to create even more profitable and in-flow launches, and clients see the same shift. The more fun you have and the more you honour yourself, the more money you make. There is tons of evidence on this.

Clients often ask me how I achieve goals if I don't use the SMART (specific, measurable, achievable, realistic and time-bound) guideline. For some, SMART goals feel aligned, but for most visionaries it creates too much of an attachment, can be restrictive, and sometimes causes disappointment for not reaching it. Who wants to be realistic anyway? I choose to believe that anything is possible, that the unrealistic is realistic, and that anything can be achieved through quantum leaps. It just takes going out and creating the life we dream of living and knowing that we are limitless.

When creating your dream life, it's crucial to understand that the Universe responds to alignment. Are you energetically aligned to the $10K+ month or whatever your goal is? Are your thoughts, beliefs, actions and energy aligned? When you are in alignment with your soul's authentic purpose, what is meant for you can drop in.

Journal Prompts

- Are you aligned with the service(s) you're offering?
- Do you believe in the transformation it will create for your soul clients?
- Are you excited and aligned with the way you are sharing your message?

The Universe doesn't respond to linear timelines, so why limit yourself with set dates? This could be a full chapter, but the purpose is to raise your awareness to the fact that there isn't a one-size-fits-all approach to setting and achieving goals.

Reaching a particular goal or not reaching it has nothing to do with your self-worth. You are worthy as you are.

The most important thing is uncovering what you want and *why* you actually want it. When we release the *how* and *when,* we open up a new space of surrender and trust. Your soul already knows what it wants to create. Generally, it's your natural inclination for a particular thing or a feeling of excitement you receive when you do an activity. In other words: follow your joy and stay the course for as long as it takes to manifest!

Journal Prompts

- What sets your soul on fire?
- What do you really love creating or doing that you're not allowing yourself to?
- What are things you're obsessed with that you could speak about all day?

When I work with clients, I look at their Human Design and their energy type to help me determine how best to work with them. Some clients need routine and structure, others feel constricted by that. Some are specific manifestors (they want to plan out exact details), while others are non-specific manifestors (more focused on a general idea or feeling). Having an individualised approach to setting goals and achieving them is *so* important. (If you feel called to learn more about Human Design, look into *www.jovianarchive.com/get_your_chart*).

I love connecting to the thoughts, words, energy and actions of the version of me that already has what I want, while letting what is meant for me delight and surprise me. I will embody the version of me that already has $200K+ cash months, but I won't focus on the specifics or details, which often keeps me thinking small.

- When I set goals, I look at the **toward principle of motivation** (moving towards what you want). *How do I want to feel when I am creating something? How will it feel when I have X number of* *clients and their lives are shifting? How will it feel to have a community of women that I get to support in a sisterhood? How will it feel when I eat healthily and move my body?*

- Most of us operate using **away from principles of motivation** (moving away from something you don't want). "I have to make this sale so that I don't have to return to my corporate job," or "I have to get 20 clients so I look like I am legitimate." The goals are set from a space of *should, have to,* or *must.* From this place, the action is then action with a means to an end, rather than being in flow or aligned.

What if you started to focus on:

I get to…

I feel aligned with adding…

I want to feel…

I always connect into how I want to *feel.* Starting with what makes me happy and excites me has shifted the way I work in my business.

A simple shift from "I **have to** create content or show up" to "I **get to** create content and show up" has been amazing for my motivation. I get to create that sales page, I get to have that sales call, I get to have a day filled with client sessions, etc. These are incredible blessings in our life that we tend to take for granted.

When I'm considering something new, I ask myself: *can I see myself doing this in 30+ years and still enjoying it?* If the answer is yes, it stays. If it drains the life out of me, it goes. Of course, I reserve the right to pivot and shift as I desire, but it helps me move from short term to longer term thinking. Remember, you get to create your dream business on *your* terms. Your business is not a fad diet filled with rules—it is about setting yourself up for consistency, sustainability and reliability.

Create your business around your life, not your life around your business.

Soul Reflection

- What do I love doing in my business?
- What do I dislike doing? What can I outsource?
- What social media platforms do I love?
- What am I doing that doesn't feel aligned?

If you hate Facebook Live, don't do it. If you hate doing sales calls, don't do them. If you hate LinkedIn, leave it alone. There is a beautiful and aligned business model that energises you, excites you, and allows you to feel vibrant. You just have to listen to your inner guidance.

THE POWER OF INTENTION

In breathwork and all of my coaching sessions, I ask clients to connect with their intention for the session. The intention may be to release emotional blocks, open the heart to receiving love, or to receive clarity on something. Intention has been incredible for directing my own personal practice to allow guidance to come through.

Everything that happens in the Universe starts with intention. A goal is linked to a desired outcome and is created from the mind in a logical way. An intention is an energetic starting point in its purest form for your goal. It's that powerfully authentic vow that comes from your core. It goes deeper than the mind and comes from a state of pure awareness. Intentions are best set from a heart space and from inner guidance.

INTENTION-SETTING RITUAL

- Close your eyes and meditate on the intention. Put your hand on your heart and allow your awareness to expand. Meditating on it and connecting afterwards is a powerful way to create intentions. After meditating, our mind is more connected to the quantum field of infinite possibility and our truth is revealed.
- Connect into your truth without the fears and what others may think. Intention is far more powerful when it comes from contentment for what we have in the present moment rather than from scarcity or a need to fix. Understand that you can create whatever you desire in this lifetime and you can choose and decide how things will happen for you.
- Practice detachment: let go of your rigid attachment to a specific result and live in the wisdom of uncertainty. When nothing is certain, anything is possible. Have faith that everything will work out as it meant to, then let go and allow opportunities and openings to come your way.
- Let the Universe support you. After detaching, I always say: "Thank you Universe for my great abundance. I love how you delight and surprise me." Let the Universe do the heavy lifting as you show up in faith knowing that magic and miracles are

your birthright. *It is always this or better.* The Universe is never testing or punishing you, it is always conspiring for you. The Universe doesn't owe you anything—in fact, it isn't even delivering something to you. Anything that is meant for you is already in your energetic field. You are the Universe.

A couple years ago, Shaun and I went away to a game reserve in South Africa. On the first day, I set the intention that we would see giraffes on the trip, detaching and allowing myself to be delighted and surprised. They hadn't seen them for a few weeks in the reserve, but I believed that I would see them on this trip. On the last day, as we were leaving, I told Shaun that I was a bit sad that we didn't see them yet, but that I had a powerful feeling that we would see them on the drive back. A hundred kilometres from the game reserve, there were 11 giraffes on the side of the road.

Of course, I have manifested incredible things above and beyond a giraffe sighting, but this example shows how we may not receive it in the time we want but that it is *always* showing up for us. People often question why they haven't manifested what they want. If you've asked yourself this question too, here are some follow-up questions I'd like you to ask yourself:

- Have you set a powerful intention?
- Are your thoughts in alignment with your feelings? Say you want something but may not believe that it is possible. I believed 100% that I would see giraffes.
- Are you staying the course?

- ▷ Is it safe for you to receive what you want now? If you feel tired, burnt out and exhausted, putting more clients and stress on top of that won't be a good idea.
- ▷ Are you detaching and allowing instead of trying to force and push?
- ▷ If you allowed the Universe to support you fully, how would that feel?

It is *as easy* to manifest bigger things as it is to manifest a giraffe sighting.

Play with the realm of possibility. Have fun!

GIVING YOURSELF GRACE IN THE GROWTH

Vanessa "Impatient" Hallick. Honestly, *impatient* may as well have been my middle name. If things didn't happen now or yesterday, I would want to give up. When things felt hard, I'd lose interest.

I now know that I can do anything with joy and flow, but it is a choice I have to make.

Living in a space of "why hasn't it happened yet?" and hyper-focusing on what hasn't worked, blocks you from allowing that which you desire to show up in your reality. As a CEO, of course you must take time assessing what worked, what didn't work, and what you would do differently moving forward. But you cannot change the past, and beating yourself up for not creating something serves literally no purpose.

My old reality looked like this: exhausting tantrums when things weren't going my way. Going into masculine overdrive when things weren't working— pushing, hustling and going harder. My new reality looks like this: I lean into the feminine, and surrender to receive. When things aren't working, I unplug from work. I take Apollo for a walk, spend time with Shaun, nap, or dance. I have learned that pushing does not result in results. It does the opposite. You don't attract what you *do* and how hard you work—you attract what you feel and believe. When you take aligned action from this space of faith, magic and miracles can drop in. Manifesting requires faith and surrender. If you give up when the going gets tough or want to throw in the towel at the first sign of adversity, it is unlikely that you will create a new reality. Stay the course, but do it with fun, and embrace the journey of what you get to do in this lifetime.

Realising the "shadow side" of impatience as well as embracing the power of it, has helped me truly know myself. When I started to recognise and understand my patterns, it felt like a never-ending process of excavating anger and fear. I remember wanting to feel happy and just let everything go, and I was even impatient in that pursuit! I wanted to get rid of the trauma and yuck feelings, rather than feeling and embracing them. At this stage, I believed that there was something wrong with me and in doing the inner work as fast as possible I would finally be there. It wasn't until I fully embraced that "shadow" and felt the deep pain and trauma around why I didn't feel safe to trust when my manifestations would come through, that I was able to lean into surrender.

I don't have to get impatient, but when I'm obsessed and excited about something, it always shows up.

When you feel excited and in love with the work you get to do, your soul clients are magnetised to you.

The next time things aren't showing up, instead of:

"Why aren't all the spaces for my programs filled up already? I must be terrible at this. No one wants this. I should give up."

Try:

"I trust that the right people always arrive at the right time. Any goal I set is always achieved when I show up, speak my truth and take aligned action."

Ask yourself daily:

- **What would my thoughts, beliefs, energy and actions be if I already had X?**

Instead of pushing through and initiating more, as the world and most programs tell you to do, honour yourself and ask yourself what you need *right now* to take care of yourself. Sometimes, we need to slow down to speed up and sometimes we need to lean into the discomfort of growth. Sometimes we need to allow ourselves to pivot, let go and shift.

Slow down to listen to the whispers of your soul.

Make sure to celebrate as much as possible on this entrepreneurial journey. Allow fun and pleasure to infuse every day, in and out of your business. I'm not a firm believer in waiting for a particular goal to be reached to celebrate: every day is a celebration. You are alive on this planet, at this particular point in history—that is a gift.

Paid To Be You Reminder

This is a reminder that you are whole and there isn't one thing that needs to fall into place to make you so. This is about opening your eyes to your own brilliance and recognising that everything you ever needed is already within you. It is about shifting your level of consciousness and embracing that anything is possible. It is about becoming an observer of your thoughts and understanding your patterns and habits, rather than berating yourself or waiting for something to be healed to be able to do something.

This is one of my favourite quotes:

"You aren't a ten-dollar bill in last winter's coat pocket. You are also not lost. Your true self is right there, buried under cultural conditioning, other people's opinions, and inaccurate conclusions you drew as a kid that became your beliefs about who you are. "Finding yourself" is actually returning to yourself."

— EMILY MCDOWELL

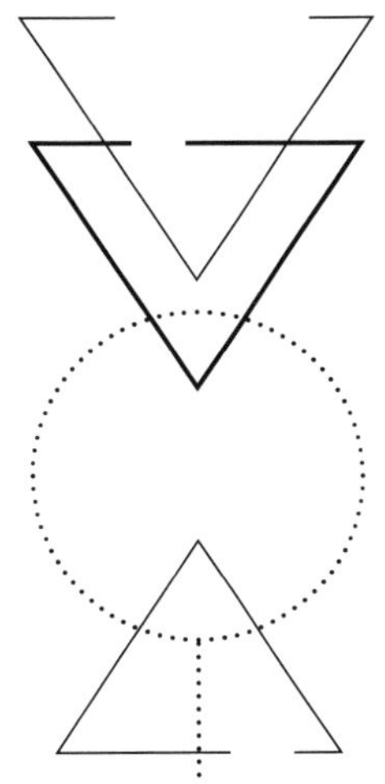

Slow down to listen to the whispers of your soul.

Success On Your Terms

I'm an Intuitive Business Mentor and Life Coach. When I first started my coaching biz, I was still stuck in the corporate mindset: that I had to look, talk, act and be a certain way, focusing only on the strategy, systems and output. This stopped me from originally believing that I could be paid to be me.

I very quickly started disliking my business. I had essentially created a corporate environment for myself even though the whole point of leaving corporate was that it had made me extremely miserable. I wanted to break out from the mould and I craved freedom — freedom to fully be me, freedom to utilise all my gifts (not just my analytical, strategic and logical mind), freedom to work from wherever and whenever I wanted to. The turning point was a low moment where I wanted to quit my business, even though I absolutely loved helping others build a wildly profitable and thriving business through strategy, mindset, inner work and energetics. *Instead of giving up, I decided to live the next year as though success was inevitable as long as I was fully myself.*

Vanessa is wonderfully encouraging and supportive! One of her missions is for women to unleash themselves so that they can be paid to be themselves! Vanessa lovingly helped guide, support and encourage me to create a program that I was excited about and to break free from the "shoulds", "have-tos" and "musts". Her programs are a beautiful blend of love, energy, breathwork, meditation and strategy — taking a completely holistic approach! I have really loved being part of her program!

PATRICIA AUER

Join her private Facebook group:
www.facebook.com/groups/thefeclub

chapter 4

Consciously Creating Your Dream Life

"I surrender to You who I am, what I have, and what I do. May my life and talents be used in whatever way serves You best. I surrender to You my failures and any pain still in my heart. I surrender to You my successes and the hopes that they may contain. May the Light of Your Love shine deep within my heart and extend through me to bless the world."

— MARIANNE WILLIAMSON

Until I was 30 years old, I was unconscious. I was governed by time, the environment around me, and my body. These are all illusions and constructs we create to make sense of the world. Everything around us is simply a reflection of our internal world.

I was constantly fixated on doing the "right" thing. I was working to pay the bills and to shop— oh, how I loved to shop and feel extremely guilty for it. Exercise and eating healthy was punishment and to weigh a certain amount on the scale. I obsessively weighed myself, pinched my fat in disgust, and felt unattractive. I was completely drained from my corporate job, and it was no surprise that I had bad acne and barely any self-love. I felt separate and disconnected from others and the spirit realm. I had severe anxiety and adrenal fatigue that I wasn't conscious of because I was so disconnected from myself and my body. I was on auto-pilot and stuck in my mind. I thought that this was *just the way life is.*

My current reality is proof that you can change, your old habits can shift, and you can create a business on your own terms. I currently work with the best clients in the world, all of whom pay me for my authentic gifts and skills. That reality exists for you, too.

Through conscious creation and taking action to change your inner belief system, and thus your outer world, you can change the environment around you for the better. Ultimately, though, as you discovered about manifestation in Chapter 3, the key factor will always be trust and surrender. There are no punishments, no negative tests. Of course, some things you think you want won't come through. When something doesn't work out, I remind myself that something even better is on its way. And I have *so much* evidence of that in my life.

Big disappointments lead to changes in your path. Maybe your partner breaks up with you, and you meet your soulmate right after. Perhaps there's a job you don't get, leading you onto the path of following your purpose. Look at your life. Can you recall moments where something that you thought you wanted didn't work out, but instead something even better happened?

There are *so many* blessings, take a moment to see them. It's not easy, but it's crucial.

When things happen out of our control, it can trigger a panic response. Often we get obsessed with the future, or a specific goal working out exactly as we envision it. There's no room for flexibility, flow or magic. I've had times when I've been fixated on the future with increasing impatience for it not happening now (or yesterday). I've had times where I've been so upset about a disappointment or a "loss," that I've missed the even better opportunity that presented itself right in front of my face. Impatience and trying to control the outcome of our life stops us from truly enjoying the present moment and actually *stops us* from receiving.

The Reticular Activating System (RAS) is a bundle of nerves at our brainstem that filters out unnecessary information so the important stuff gets through. The RAS is the reason you learn a new word and then start hearing it everywhere. When you start to see success online and people having 6-figure launches, you may start to see it everywhere. It is also why if you focus on something negative like how hard it is to make money, or how your programs aren't resonating, you'll start to see that in your reality. When you focus on people not liking you, evidence will appear to support this too.

The amazing thing is, we can direct our attention and train our brains to see more of what we want in our reality. The RAS also does a magical thing where it brings triggers into your environment so you can have the opportunity to heal them. If something is triggering you on a subconscious (or conscious) level, it will likely pop into your world over and over until you face it. The next time something comes into your external environment that triggers you, consider the following:

- Why am I seeing this today?
- What part of me is triggered by this? Why am I triggered?
- What am I not owning or seeing is meant for me?
- What do I need to release?

The other day, a client messaged me and said she was jealous about my photoshoot. I told her that the jealousy was there to show her it is meant for her, and it was time to book her shoot! Instead of letting the comparison make you feel less than, try turning it into a positive: "If she can do it, so can I!"

When a post triggers you, ask yourself how you want to respond to the trigger. You can either spiral about what you haven't yet accomplished (or what you don't have) or look at what that person has that is a reflection of what you're ready to access in *your* energetic field.

The RAS is quite simple to re-train. Spend a few minutes a day looking around you and writing down or acknowledging everything you are grateful for. Spend a minute or two holding your heart in appreciation for whatever you can be appreciative of—no matter how big or small. Breathe it in, start to resonate at the frequency of joy, and be aware of how you feel. These will start to direct the RAS on more of what you do want, and less of what you don't.

Appreciate the simple things in life—the blissful coffee in the morning, the new client that is incredible, the hugs with your partner, the body that does so much for us, or the walk outside. The simple act of breathing is such an incredible thing.

You consciously create your reality. There are no coincidences of what you see, the people that say things to you, or what appears in your daily life. Everything is happening for your growth and evolution. When you pay attention to the signs and recognise that whatever you see is a mirror of your inner world, you grow massively, profoundly, and powerfully. You get less triggered, and feel more at peace.

Ask yourself:

- Why is this happening for my growth and evolution?
- What could the gift in the growth be?

We have millions of thoughts coming into our subconscious and a small fraction of those can actually be processed by the conscious brain. Think of how many sounds, smells, tastes and feelings exist right now in this current moment as you sit here reading this book. The key function of your conscious mind is to distort, generalise and delete to make sense of all the information.

This is why we live in a black-and-white, good-and-bad, and either/or society. We judge others for not being like us and doing what we think they should do with the information we have. We create labels and titles to make sense of the world around us. It's common to get fixated on the idea that when you do X, you'll get X outcome. The paradigm of doing things for a specific outcome is what keeps us on the treadmill of misery, self-doubt, and ultimately, unhappiness. It's also why people get fixated on their job title, the idea that they need X amount of clients to be able to feel X or do X. The desire to reach external goals for internal validation.

At this point, I think you know what I'm going to say: It doesn't work like that! How you get clients and how successful your business is is about the totality of who you are, your own belief in what you offer, the energetic capacity you have, and how turned on you are about what you sell.

Passion sells. Your energy sells. Not a pretty title or one-liner—that distracts you from your truth. Alright, I said it. Now that that's off my chest, we can move on!

3D CONSCIOUSNESS

Your brain is only as powerful as the being that operates it, it loves the path of least resistance and the familiar, but you're smarter than that. Question, observe, and see the gift in what is being presented to you. Your mind is a powerful ally, when you understand that you have the power over what you think.

Life is not black and white. It's a rainbow of colours, multifaceted and multidimensional! (And who would even want it to be black and white? Boring!)

However, it's easier to create order in our brain if things are black and white. It's easier to go through life with a familiar program based on your childhood conditioning. Why do you think most of the population acts like unhealed children? Unless you become consciously aware of your thoughts and behaviours, essentially, that's what you are.

Part of being paid to be you, is no longer allowing your 6-year-old self to run your business.

I remember the first time I started questioning things and went against what I was taught to believe and what I *thought* was my truth. It was disturbing and extremely challenging. However, we can only do better when we know better, and you owe it to yourself and clients to do the best you can with the gifts you have.

Black-and-white thinking keeps us stuck in 3D consciousness—which, in other words, is the state of being unconscious. It isn't easy work to shift into consciousness and awareness, but it's incredible! This section of the book is about creating an awareness for you to see what's possible and how to start shifting.

3D consciousness is viewing things from a purely physical state. You are seen as an individual that is separate from others. Life feels like "survival of the fittest" and you are identified by the way you look, the job you have, the car you drive, and the people you surround yourself with. You feel fearful about missing out or not having enough. Things are perceived as being good or bad, and life is a competition. There is not enough for everyone and some people have to miss out. Fulfilment is found in making money and social status. Your thoughts have no power over your reality and what comes your way in life is simply a coincidence.

Sound familiar?

SHIFTING FROM 4D TO 5D CONSCIOUSNESS

In 2015, I read *Leveraging The Universe* by Mike Dooley, and I had my first moment of awareness about how thoughts become things, and that you get to create your reality. I started moving from being a victim of my world and situation to understanding that the Universe is conspiring *for me* and my evolution. I created an awareness around everything that was happening, and started seeing signs, symbols and synchronicities in my world. I started viewing everything around me as happening for my growth and evolution.

4D is the state of consciousness where you're aware, but still living in the shadows projected from the dense plane of 3D. 4D is a canopy of light that gets murky from projected shadows, and as we start to integrate all parts of us, we open the portal for higher dimensions. It is essential for integration and healing to take place in order to access 5D. We need to create an awareness and understanding that polar opposites (good/bad, right/wrong) are not mutually exclusive and can coexist within us.

To move through 4D into 5D consciousness, it is important to:

- Heal the emotional body through identifying, expressing and releasing anger, rage and grief. To be able to hold the full range of emotions without assigning *good* or *bad* value to anything.
- Release drama created through unhealed emotions and inner child wounds.
- Return to unconditional love for ourselves and others and to open our heart centre.
- Release judgment of ourselves and others.
- Get to know and have compassion for the shadow self, and integrate the shadow so that you can experience a new level of love and wholeness.
- Integrate the evolved Masculine and Feminine energies and embrace your natural rhythms and cycles.

In order to be paid to be you and to be able to hold space for the healing and awakening of others, it is important to do this inner work and integration while showing up for what is important to you. *You don't need to stop everything to integrate these or escape for months — in fact most of the work and clarity comes from taking aligned actions while leaning into discomfort and observing our thoughts. It can be easy to get caught up in a perpetual cycle of needing to heal a block or limiting belief before doing something. You aren't blocked and the more you focus on it, the more it expands. You are ready to do exactly what you're called to do now.*

Living From A 5D State

The day I read about 5D consciousness in 2018, I was fascinated by how much of my life had been filled with drama, fear, exhaustion and worry. How alone I had felt in the world and how I had lived in black and white. I still go between 3D, 4D and 5D consciousness as I navigate, shift and develop a greater conscious awareness, but it opened my eyes to what was possible, the freedom we can experience, and the inner peace that is available to us. Remember that all of these levels of consciousness exist simultaneously, and it is up to us to choose whether we operate from the higher vibrational expression of self, or the shadow self.

5D State Of Consciousness

From this level of consciousness, you begin to understand that we are all one and we are all connected. Life becomes an adventure of growth and there is no such thing as good or bad. There is a higher purpose for all things and every experience holds meaning.

There are stronger feelings of love and connectedness with others, the planet and even the galaxies around us. Love and compassion is expanded and we release lack of judgement. You understand that everyone is just on their own journey.

Everyone is considered to be equal and there is a desire to live from a place of pure authenticity. You understand that your purpose is to live your truth and to seek joy.

From this state, you know that there is no competition and there is enough in the Universe for everyone. You feel overwhelming emotions of love and compassion for life, Mother Earth, and the stars.

Your intuition is extremely strong and you feel connected to angelic beings.

This dimension is characterised by high levels of creativity, unconditional love, deep empathy and intuitive ability and having the desire to help with the awakening and healing of others on this planet. Your cells start to speed up as they vibrate faster allowing us to manifest faster and shift.

Earth is 3D, so the key is staying grounded in this physical space while being in 5D consciousness.

ALLOWING YOUR NEGATIVE THOUGHTS TO GUIDE YOUR EXPANSION

You may have thought patterns that are not fully aligned to your bigger vision. That's common. As we expand, grow and evolve, self-limiting beliefs may come up. It is what we do with them, not whether we still have them. During my Neuro Linguistic Programming (NLP) training, I was taught to look at thoughts this way: if you're looking into a stream (the infinite beauty of the world) and you see a dead leaf (a negative thought), you can choose to focus on the dead leaf, run down the river, and follow it. Alternatively, you can bring your attention back to the life-giving stream which is far bigger and more powerful. Starting to create that discipline in your mind is *so* important as we recognise that we have power over what we think. If we try to ignore the dead leaf, we may easily become fixated on it. However, if we acknowledge it, identify the gift in it, and consciously bring our attention back to what we want to focus on, we can create more of what we want to see in our reality.

Everything in your reality (including thoughts) are guiding you closer to your next evolution. Don't fight expansion and growth! Lean into the gift. Start to be the observer of your thoughts, instead of berating yourself for having them or being afraid of negative thought patterns.

People have this idea that when you reach a certain level of income, the fears and limiting beliefs magically disappear. They think that when you get *there*, it's all rainbows and unicorns, and you become fearless. The truth is, what used to scare me is not as scary, but I still have doubts when I launch a new program, when I write a book, when I hire a new team member, and even when I do a Facebook Live.

The fears are showing you that you're alive, you're doing big things, and that what you're creating is meant for you. Fears are also friends! Speak to them, take out a chair and listen to their wisdom. Don't shun them to the corner.

When I launch a new program, there are always fears as I put it out into the world. I used to run away from this discomfort. Now I know that it's my moment of truth. Either I lean in and follow through, or I walk the other way. The programs I've been meant to launch (that are in the highest alignment with me) have always been created and successful.

Whatever is meant for you *will not leave.*

When you launch something new, the fear, the discomfort and the courage start to shape you into the version of you that can hold the sacred space that is required. Lean in and learn the lessons of that expansion.

"Oh, hey fear! Thanks for showing me that this is meant for me! I love you! I appreciate your wisdom and thank you for protecting me, but I am so excited about this and I am going for it."

Hear the fears cheering you on!

Soul Reflection

- What would faith and love choose?
- What are the fears telling me?
- What would happen if I let the fears guide me?
- Is what I am desiring to create true to me and my higher self?

ALLOWING YOURSELF TO BE GUIDED AND SUPPORTED ON THIS JOURNEY

For so long, I felt alone and unsupported. It felt like it was me against the world. I felt vulnerable, disconnected, and as if life was *so* fragile. I felt that at any moment the rug could be pulled from underneath me and that my worth in the world was determined by how much I achieved.

Burnout gave me the gift of softening to strengthen. Having to slow down, to feel, to embody, to take time in nature to reconnect, and to listen to guidance moment-to-moment. I stopped trying to frantically plan things and instead honoured myself deeply and received guidance and support from the spirit and angelic realm. Before a call, training, or Facebook Live, I set an intention, take a moment to connect into the infinite support of the Universe, and say:

"Spirit guides, angels and ancestors of the highest truth and order please guide me and allow me to be a channel for the highest good of humanity. Use me as a messenger and vessel to shift those around me."

We live in a vibrational Universe and everything that we desire is at a vibrational frequency. It is why we need to master the art of allowing, detaching, surrendering, and taking the spiritually-aligned action that you are guided to take. It is internal—everything works through you as a messenger. It isn't about asking for guidance from anything external, but tapping into your higher wisdom. Listen to your inner knowing.

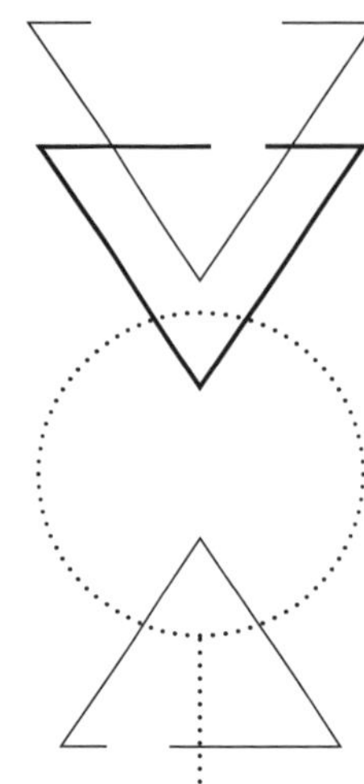

What the world needs now is feeling, honouring your natural cycle, firm boundaries and taking action in alignment with your soul blueprint.

You can't fake a high frequency by doing more. More morning routines, more crystals, or more frantic shifting of your state. What the world needs now is feeling, honouring your natural cycle, firm boundaries and taking action in alignment with your soul blueprint.

CONSCIOUSLY CREATING YOUR DREAM DAY

"Today is another incredible day filled with magic and miracles. I am so excited for all that will flow into my life and be created."

Every morning, I wake up and repeat these words.

You get to consciously create your day. Write out how you want the day to go, the fun and pleasure you will have, and how you want to feel. Fill your day with more of what brings you joy, listen in to what you need, and create more pleasure in the mundane.

Fun and pleasure is not reserved for when you're "good," e.g. when you've finished your work, hit a big goal, or signed on a new client. You don't have to eat your greens before you have dessert! See how much fun you can fill your day with.

▷ **If I were to fill my day with more fun and pleasure in my life and work I would...**

Content writing is an area that most online entrepreneurs find tedious, but it's one of my favourite things. I create a total pleasure practice around it. I set a day aside for writing and creating. I start my day beautifully with a forest walk with Apollo and a gorgeous breakfast. When I'm writing, I clear my desk and have some dark chocolate and tea. Coming into the present with everything is so important. Sometimes I receive clear guidance to share something—I go with it, trusting that *I am the message.*

I've shifted my thinking from "I have to do this" to "I get to do this."

I get to write and get paid to write.

I get to share my message with the world and impact lives.

I get to have incredible calls with clients from around the world.

PAID TO BE YOU MANTRA

Allow yourself to embrace and receive the pleasure of life. We so often learn that there has to be sacrifice. What if you dropped that notion and allowed yourself to receive?

I receive the pleasure

I receive the fun

I receive the joy

Oh, Universe, I love the way you constantly delight and surprise me

Mmmm, delicious

BRINGING YOUR DREAM LIFE INTO REALITY

For most of my life, I didn't realise that I could create my reality. I was afraid of setting big goals or asking for what I wanted because I didn't want to be disappointed. Since starting my business, I have been overwhelmed with the magic that exists and seen with my own eyes how much can change.

We don't need to be fixated on the details, but if you allow yourself to think big, connect into infinite possibilities, and know that your soul desires are there for a reason... you will see the magic present itself.

One of my incredible clients mentioned she wanted to purchase a holiday home in Florida for her and her family. It was a soul desire and something she was incredibly excited about, but she felt guilty about wanting it. She asked if it was wasteful or greedy. I asked her to consider how she felt when she thought about being in the holiday house with her family. Her voice instantly shifted as she told me of the memories, delight and pleasure the family would experience. When we honour our soul desires, the way we create and show up also shifts.

She created this as a soul goal and allowed herself to create, show up, and sell as if the home was already hers.

A few months later, she emailed to say she had just put the down payment on the house and that she was *so excited*. Not only had she created this, but she was experiencing more pleasure, joy and fun within her work because of it.

Give yourself permission to want what you want without judgement. Without creating rules for how money should or must be used. Give yourself permission to honour your juicy and delicious desires.

These things wouldn't excite you if they were not meant for you. We don't need to be fixated on receiving them, but know that whatever you see in your mind is already created, and go about your life knowing that you are divinely provided for. Because you always are.

8 STEPS TO MANIFEST ANYTHING YOU WANT

Grab your journal and your favourite beverage, and while working through these steps, *do not hold back*. Be unapologetic. Get creative. Use colours, pictures, or whatever makes you feel excited. I find on sales calls when I ask about a potential client's bigger vision, I get a watered-down vision. When we work together and we really go there, it's incredible to see the energy and light beaming out of them. Go there now!

Be unapologetic about what you desire and what sets your soul on fire. Give yourself permission to create your business around your life—not the other way around. Give yourself full permission to decide what you will create while leaving room for even more magic.

This is meant to be a fun, playful and expansive process. Not a needy and creepy vibe. Know that it always shows up, but detach from the timeline.

1. Declare exactly what you want

I've always found that my reality is even more incredible when I allow it to unfold. A few years ago, I couldn't have imagined this life I have now. You will always be delighted and surprised, but allowing yourself to start to get creative and reconnect to the possibilities is a fun way to expand your energetic capacity to receive.

Get excited, and remember: you get to consciously create your reality.

- **What does your ideal day look like?**

  Write it as if it is already your reality.

  What is the first thing you do when you wake up?

  How do you start your day?

  How do you feel as you move through the day?

  What do you want to fill your day with?

- **What is it that you really desire in all areas of your life including health, wealth, relationships, and business?**

What we need to remember is that it gets to be even better than this, but this is a starting point. E.g. Do you want to travel the world, speak on stage, publish a book? What is your biggest vision? Name it and claim it!

If you find this difficult, ask yourself: why am I not admitting to myself what I truly want? Will it create change we're scared of? Upset people we love? Name it and face it.

Example Soul Affirmations:

I am making X amount in my business with absolute ease! Money is overflowing. It's the way it is.

I am impacting millions of lives with my message.

I am a bestselling author.

I show up, speak my truth, have fun and I am paid to be me.

My relationship is growing in love and connection.

I eat what I want and move daily. My body is healthy and sexy. I love taking care of my vessel and I feel beautiful in my own skin.

- ▷ If you were to give yourself permission to have it ALL, what would that look like in each area?
- ▷ What do you need to allow time and energy for in each of these areas?
- ▷ How can you bring more pleasure and joy to all areas of your life?

Remember that time is in ample supply and we always have more than enough for what is important to us. Time isn't linear like we see it.

If you're doing things that are not aligned and that drain your energy, this is also a great space to release those things. Contrary to what most of us believe growing up, honouring yourself and putting yourself first is essential. If we constantly sacrifice, over-give and try to fix others, we deplete our energy. Fill up your cup first and do what you love—you'll have more energy to serve others from this space.

Often we say that we don't have time or money for what we want. If you're pushing off your dreams with excuses, it's time to start saying that out loud. "This is not a priority right now." How does that change the way you think? Is it because your goals aren't in alignment with your soul? Or is it because of fear? Only you can answer that.

- Goal that's out of alignment: I should work out every day at the gym because that's what fit people do.

- New aligned goal: I want to dance, go into nature, and will commit to two days at the gym/week because I know resistance training is great for bone density and muscle mass.
- Goal that's out of alignment: I should do a Facebook Live every day so my followers see how committed I am.
- New aligned goal: I would like boundaries around my social media use, so I will commit to three days/week where I go on social media. My followers will respect my content and know that I am taking time for me.

Moving your goals and actions into alignment will get you on your path to being paid to be you. Think about the kind of money you'd need to have the life you truly desire.

▷ What do you desire to be making every month in your business? Think big, this isn't a time to play small.

2. Why do you want what you want?

That which is truly aligned will be able to drop in when it is something that is *actually* aligned to your soul's blueprint.

Think about your authentic desires, and tap into your soul.

▷ Why do you want those things?

> E.g. I want multiple 7-figures so that I can make a massive impact in the lives of others and be able to give back freely to causes close to my heart. I want to be able to take care of myself at the highest level so I have the energy to serve more clients. I want to be able to expand into this version of myself that holds wealth at that level.

E.g. I want a beautiful home because when I work and live in a beautiful space, I feel expanded. I want to be able to have a gorgeous space to host in-person intensives.

This is not to justify what you desire (wanting it is simply enough!), but this helps to connect more with your *why* and determine whether it is something that really is *your* version of success.

3. To normalise that vision, let's go even bigger

- If that vision was already done, what is the vision beyond the vision?
- What would you create then?
- What would be possible for you?

Remember that there are infinite possibilities and that you *do* get to consciously create your reality!

Connect into how it will feel to have your vision beyond the vision. Close your eyes for a few moments and visualise this vision already having happened.

- What does it feel like?
- What are you wearing?
- How are the soul clients you are working with shifting?

4. Manifesting from the subconscious and opening your channels to receive

Affirmations and visualizations are wonderful ways to connect to our conscious mind. We have to remember, though, that we manifest from the *subconscious*. If there is a misalignment between what you want and your beliefs around whether that's possible for you (aka. you don't truly believe that you can have it), it won't be able to come into your reality. It's simple: if you believed it was possible, it would have already shown up in your reality. We need to look at what the subconscious belief patterns are that are not in alignment with what you want.

▷ What self-limiting beliefs do you have that this vision is not possible?

> *E.g. no one in my family has ever done that; I'm not great with money; My programs are not worth what I want to charge.*

▷ What is the truth and evidence that this is possible for you?

> *E.g. I now manage my finances and have an accountant that helps me. The money I spent was for big investments for the growth of my business. I know that money is in infinite supply. I know there are no wrong decisions when it comes to money.*

▷ Why is it not safe to receive this?

> *E.g. If I make more money then I will have less freedom in my life. I won't have time to look after myself.*

- What am I getting from NOT manifesting what I say I want?

  E.g. Maybe you want to quit your corporate job but you have a lot of friends there. You are more afraid that when you quit your job you'll have no friends. On some level you may self-sabotage so that you still keep the friends.

  E.g. You may say you want to make enough money to have your partner quit his job but you're more afraid of him being under your feet at home or you're afraid that you don't want to be solely responsible for the income.

- Why is it more safe?

  E.g. When I make more money, I will outsource the things that I don't want to do.

  If my husband/partner quits, he can focus on what he really wants. We can hire someone to support him. If it doesn't work, we are no worse off, he could go back to a job. It isn't an outcome I want, but I would rather try. What is the worst that can happen? What is the best that can happen?

- What do I need to release?

  E.g. I won't end up alone if I make $100K months; My relationship won't fall apart if I make more.

- What are your new beliefs?

  E.g. Making more money does not equal less freedom. I know that working longer hours does not equate to more money. If I were to create my business without sacrifice and in total alignment, I would...

Here are some examples of powerful affirmations that you can repeat. Or make your own!

I am a powerful money magnet.

I have everything I need to create a massive change in the lives of others.

My relationship will get better and better as we have more time together.

5. Feeling and embodying the version of you that already has what you want

We are emotional beings and the brain doesn't know the difference between reality and imagination. We also know that based on quantum physics, this version of you that you see already exists. We can get into the feelings, emotions and gratitude now for whatever we are wanting to bring into reality.

Close your eyes, take a deep breath in for the count of four, hold for four, and release for four. Start to visualise the life you want, the home you stay in, the travel, the clients, and the money coming into your bank account. Allow every cell of your being to elevate and activate. Visualise yourself speaking your truth, sharing your message powerfully, your energy rising and the money coming into your bank account, the new payment notifications in your email and the feeling of true inner peace and bliss as you are paid to be you.

Allow yourself to feel this.

- How does your body feel? How are you showing up in the world now? How is your breathing different?

6. Meeting the version of you who has already created your bigger vision

Nothing happens without action. You can collapse timelines and create a quantum shift by aligning and showing up *now* as that version of you. It may feel uncomfortable and you may feel resistance. It is time to take action if you really want what you say you want!

- What are the thoughts, beliefs, energy and actions of the version of you that already has created your bigger vision?

  E.g. Soul clients reach out to me daily and can't wait to pay me for my services.

  I am a money magnet.

  I am happy, healthy and live in abundance.

  I am a bestselling author.

- What are the actions that come to mind to embody this version of you? Trust that you already instinctively know the actions to take to build your business.

  E.g. I am showing up powerfully on Instagram stories and offering my services.

I am hiring a virtual assistant to support me with tech in my business.

I am writing my book.

7. Have fun, creativity and pleasure in the process

We receive from the feminine energy (creativity, intuition), so allow more fun and pleasure in your life.

▷ How can I create more fun and pleasure in all areas of my life?

8. See it manifest

Stay the course and continue to show up in your life like whatever you want is already done. Follow the threads, take the leap and listen to your inner guidance. Manifesting something is simply bringing it into reality—watch how miracles and manifestations unfold in your life with ease.

STAYING CONNECTED TO YOUR BIGGER VISION ON A DAILY BASIS

- **WRITE IT**

Write it as if it is already done. Don't go creepy on yourself here—the Universe doesn't respond to being told what you want over and over. It responds to your energy and feeling. Connect with your vision and write it out with confidence like it is already done. It is! That version of you already exists!

I am incredible at what I do because I was born a miracle.

I am happy, healthy and live in abundance.

I am a bestselling author impacting millions with my message.

I am rich, hot and influential.

Keep going! Don't judge it— let whatever needs to come through, come through.

- **SPEAK IT**

  I love to speak as if it has already happened: "I am so excited for my 20 or more new clients!" or "I'm so grateful that we're buying our dream home." I love to say these things to Shaun and have these conversations in faith that it is already taken care of, no drama.

- **SEE IT AND VISUALISE IT DAILY**

  Take time to visualise and get into the feeling of whatever you want already being in your reality. How does it feel to already have the life you want (or even better) now?

- **MOVE INTO YOUR VISION AND DANCE WITH LIFE**

  Dancing with music while closing my eyes (often naked) is one of my favourite ways to connect into my truth and shift my energy. It raises my energy, frequency and vibration.

  When we dance unrestrained, our spirit takes over and with each movement we connect back to the harmony and flow of life. Put on some music, dance, move, and fall into the frequency of life. By doing this for just a few minutes, your body will start to move intuitively. I often find I receive the most powerful guidance and content through dancing. If dancing is not your thing, move in a way that feels aligned for you to shift your energy. You can't create a new reality and experience without changing your energy first. You also can't create a solution to a problem with the same mind that created it.

If I need guidance on my next steps or clarity on something I am creating, often I will set an intention (without attachment) prior to dancing.

Often the best ideas can come through during exercise, a walk, or even a shower. Science backs this by showing how the brain lights up and the volume of the hippocampus is increased. I often get asked how I get so many ideas for content; a lot of what I write comes from what comes through on a walk or hike in the forest.

Everything is energy, and we can create a new reality by shifting our vibration, energy and frequency. Not only is exercise amazing, but the benefits for your health, wealth and happiness are powerful. I used to only do it for punishment or to lose weight, so be mindful of the energy behind it!

WHAT TO DO IF WHAT YOU WANT ISN'T SHOWING UP

Now you know exactly what you want, and you've connected into your unique version of success. Remember, we manifest from the subconscious. Life needs to look as good on the inside as it does on the outside. In order to manifest, we need to focus on the spiritual, mental, emotional, physical and energetic bodies. When we embody true peace, joy, and feel deserving of our desires, the physical manifestations simply... show up. But it can't happen until you know that you are worthy of what you want. Fullstop.

In 2019, just after burning out, I wanted 20 new clients in *Supercharge Your Success*. I showed up and took action, but on a subconscious level I knew I wasn't ready for that number. When it didn't happen, I had a meltdown. My inner dialogue went a bit like this:

"How can you teach others to get clients if you're not even doing it? You're terrible at this. How can you do this?"

I needed to be radically honest with myself.

"Vanessa, you've just started improving your health and energetic capacity to receive! You're doing great, but you have more work to do. What is the soul-aligned goal for you?"

It wasn't about playing small, but being radically honest with myself.

We can't be disappointed with the things that didn't work out if we weren't ready for them. As a CEO, we need to be able to answer these questions honestly, without self-judgment.

- Why didn't what I want show up?
- What really happened in that launch?
- What would I do differently next time?

These questions are honest, constructive ways to look at how we can grow, instead of the barrage of negativity and berating that often happens. That negative self-talk does nothing except stop us from learning the lessons for our growth and continued success.

6 REASONS WHY WHAT YOU SAY YOU WANT HASN'T SHOWN UP (YET)

Go through them with a commitment to unlocking the reason.

1. Unapologetically claim your desires

Often we say we want more, but at the same time, we are not *deeply* owning it.

I had this with my body. I love my body now and I'm comfortable with what I look like, but simultaneously I want to look *even hotter*. Not because I have to, but because I desire to. I have years left of my life and I want to get leaner, fitter, and even healthier.

I kept self-sabotaging and giving up on the commitments I made to myself. A couple of weeks ago, I hired a personal trainer because I wanted that accountability and I love resistance training. I wanted to show up for the sessions to focus on being fitter, stronger and firmer. I wanted to lean into the discomfort of change and commit to the shift. I wanted to nourish my ability to do things that aren't easy to bring about change. A couple of sessions in, I wanted to give up—and I have previously. But, this time I realised I really wanted to continue. As we age, resistance training is powerful for bone density and being strong physically is something I love.

Looking a certain way doesn't make me more worthy. I am worthy and loved as I am. But why wouldn't I be leaner, stronger and healthier?

Honouring my desire to have an even hotter body was a decision I needed to make. The last time my body was leaner was when I burnt out. I equated looking a certain way to being sick, exhausted, and unhappy. When I realised the pattern, and that looking the way I want doesn't have to do with sacrifice, everything shifted. Finally, it was safe for me to have what I want. I move daily in a way that my body loves, I eat what my body craves and I take care of my body at the highest level.

It is time to claim it. To decide.

You don't have to sacrifice anything, but you do have to own, name and claim what you want. Unapologetically. There is nothing wrong with turning up the dial in *any* area of your life.

Journal Prompts

- Are you truly aligned and in faith that whatever you want will materialise?
- If not, what will make you feel more confident?
- What is stopping you from believing it?
- Why is it not safe to have what you want? What are you telling yourself you will lose?
- What are you not claiming you really want? What are you ready to now claim?

Understand Your Subconscious Beliefs And Nervous System

We manifest from the subconscious. Our nervous system will also stop us from taking on more than we can handle.

If you're energetically maxed out and your adrenals are shot, it wouldn't be in service to you to go from $10K months into $100K months. I have done it, but I also crashed! Your subconscious and your body are trying to keep you safe. Be honest with yourself and where you are. If it feels safe, decide to show up as that next level version of you. If you feel maxed out, you can create a conscious awareness of your language. Are you saying "I am tired" or "I feel maxed out" out loud constantly? Where can you invite yourself to create new inner dialogue? E.g. "I invite ease and exponential income growth."

If it is safe, name it, claim it, and show up like it's already done.

2. What you say you want and what you're doing isn't aligned

Often, we know the actions we need to take or the investments we need to make, but we're not actually taking them. If the aligned action is hiring someone to support you with your social media, but you're too afraid to in case it doesn't work out, you're already saying that you don't believe it will work out.

We need to take the actions of the next version of ourselves, even when they're scary. We can't expect a different reality if we keep doing what we've always done. Take calculated risks. At first, it may mean small steps as you develop more faith.

- ▷ What are the aligned actions if you already have what you wanted?
- ▷ What would faith do?
- ▷ Where are you holding yourself back right now?

3. You give up when it feels hard

Typically, when you launch a program, it isn't going to sell out off the first post. Of course, anything is possible, but things can take time. Stay the course and stay connected to your *why*. If you're connected to your purpose and your authentic *why*, you'll keep selling because you can't not. Shout it out! Yes, it may feel uncomfortable! Yes, your brain may try and convince you to quit. Keep showing up for your bigger version.

- ▷ Are you staying the course with faith? If not, what stops you?
- ▷ How can you set yourself up for staying the course?
- ▷ When things feel uncomfortable how do you respond? What shift can you take?

As a culture, we are addicted to instant gratification. Often when things don't work out as we want, we tantrum, give up, or convince ourselves we don't need it.

If you want something, commit to receiving it and staying the course for as long as it takes.

4. You're fixated on the outcome

Remember that we are manifesting for our highest good, and sometimes it isn't showing up because it truly isn't for our highest good. Having 20 new clients when you already feel exhausted wouldn't be in service to you or to others. If we want to manifest something, it is important to be grateful for what we have in the moment to allow more to drop in. Have fun and enjoy the present moment. Ask for what you want, align with it, make space for it, and let go of the outcome. Allow the Universe to delight and surprise you. Needy is creepy and it takes us out of the present moment.

- ▷ What are you grateful for in the present moment?
- ▷ How does it feel to have gratitude for what is already on its way to you?

When I was in my corporate job, I spent an entire session with my coach complaining about how terrible it was. Hearing myself on the recording made me realise how much time and energy was wasted focusing on the negative. Instead, I decided to be grateful for my job. After all, it was funding my dreams!

I wrote:

I am grateful for my corporate job because it allows me to pay for my dreams. I am grateful that I get to listen to my money audios on the way to work, while simultaneously showing up for my bigger vision.

The more grateful we are for what we have, the more we receive things to be grateful for.

5. Make space for what you want

If you want X new clients, make space, and set yourself up for that. Create space in your calendar, start to create the group, set up the agreements, write the sales page. Do whatever actions you would have in place if you already had those clients.

▷ How do you need to make space for what you want to manifest?

▷ What do you really want in your schedule?

6. Find the gift in the growth

If what you want hasn't shown up, you need to be prepared to look within. Everything that is meant for you is already in your energetic field. The moments where things don't go our way, are defining moments in our growth and evolution. That is what leads us to our bigger vision.

▷ What is the gift in this growth?

▷ What is the lesson I'm being taught?

▷ Why is this happening for my growth and evolution?

If everything always went exactly as our ego wanted, we would never grow. To allow what is already in your energetic field to drop in, your current version of you needs to learn the growth lessons.

But think about it this way: why would you receive more if you can't handle or appreciate what you already have?

For example, when a client says *no* on a sales call, if you go on a week-long emotional rollercoaster, then you're not ready to take on more clients or expand your income. Emotional intelligence is key. How would the multiple 7-figure version of you manage this situation?

When someone says *no,* it means nothing about you, your worth, or how valuable your business is. Look at where the objection is coming from: everything is a mirror of your internal world. E.g. "I would love to but I can't afford it" may be an invitation to look at where you don't believe in the investment of your program. Maybe they're just not an ideal client for you. I celebrate those that don't sign up, as I know it makes space for soul clients.

You can't do anything wrong with your soul clients!

A LOT CAN CHANGE IN YOUR LIFE

After we left Bali in 2018, Shaun and I wanted to move back to South Africa. We had been living abroad in London and Bali for over 12 years and we were excited about returning home.

Our business was started at the kitchen table in our one-bedroom flat in London. I was charging $25/hour and had tons of fears about being visible. I still cringe at the first Facebook Live I did, asking the audience to *give me hearts, give me likes.* I was desperate for approval (and sales) but I am *so* grateful I kept going and stayed the course. I have grown so much since.

When we were moving back, I wrote out my non-negotiables. Honestly, how I live now is far more incredible than I could have imagined and it just keeps on getting better. We are always guided, supported and divinely provided for when we are following our soul's purpose.

This is what I wrote at the time:

I am living close to a safe and beautiful space to walk.

I am living close to the beach.

I am living close to a spa for ultimate relaxation and self-care.

I am getting a beautiful golden retriever who is the best walking buddy.

Soul clients reach out to me daily and get excited to pay me whatever I charge.

Today, I sit in my upstairs office and can see the spa from my window. I have a stunning forest hike five minutes away from my home that has a gorgeous secluded beach at the bottom, and Apollo is the *best* walking buddy. I often get messages from new clients saying how excited they are to pay me. Shaun and I live our dream life and it just continues to get better and better. We live in an infinite and ever-expanding Universe. It is normal to want more, but equally (if not more) important to enjoy the journey and appreciate what you do have in the present moment.

"Be thankful for what you have; you'll end up having more. If you concentrate on what you don't have, you will never, ever have enough."

— OPRAH WINFREY

The more gratitude you have for the present, the more you can allow to come into your reality. It doesn't mean you have to settle or judge yourself for wanting more, because receiving more is a part of growing and evolving. It would be bizarre to think that my business and life will be exactly the same for the next 30 years. We are here to expand our income, impact and level of joy.

Reminder: You get to create your reality. You get to have it ALL. You get to have what you want for the highest good of humanity. (Remember that it's not all about you. You have a purpose on this planet, and things may not show up because they're not actually aligned for you. Surrender to the divine plan, show up for your mission and purpose, and allow the Universe to co-create with you.)

Consciously Creating Your Dream Business & Life Without Sacrifice

As a copywriter and email marketing expert, I work with female coaches and course creators in the online space. I help my clients attract the people they actually want to work with and turn their browsers into buyers.

When I reached out to Vanessa, I was a little over a year into my business, working 10-hour days, six days a week. And yet, I was barely covering my expenses.

I was thrilled to be doing the work I loved, but I knew working around the clock wasn't sustainable. I didn't see a way out.

Vanessa helped me identify the kind of projects I was really excited about working on. I found that focusing on doing more of those (instead of taking every job that came my way) allowed me to build a business that felt alive and aligned.

During the time we worked together, Vanessa helped me shift so many beliefs I had that were making my business harder than it needed to be.

I learned that the work I did helped my clients make more money and I deserved to be paid well for my expertise vs. trading time for dollars.

Sure, Vanessa helped me implement the strategies and the systems that allowed me to grow and scale my business, but more importantly, working with Vanessa changed my entire approach to business.

I no longer make decisions based on fear or lack. I'm not in a race to do more and work harder (which is a very masculine way of doing things).

I feel completely free to be who I am, knowing that I'm attracting the clients I'm meant to work with.

These days, I only take on projects and clients that feel like a great fit.

I'm 100% confident in my pricing because I know the value of my work and how it changes my clients' businesses.

Because of that, I have more time to explore and create, honoring my physical, emotional, and spiritual well-being in the process.

CHRISTY CEGELSKI, Copywriter.
Find Christy here: www.christycegelski.com

chapter 5

Mindset Of Upleveling

In June 2018, I was on cloud nine. I rang in a $100K sales week, I was feeling energised, the business was booming, I had eight team members, my body was reshaping and losing weight with ease, my sex life was amazing, and my relationship with Shaun was incredible.

And then came the crash.

The next month, I made less than $7K for the full month, I was suicidal, depressed, burnt out and anxious. A deep wave of negativity had engulfed me and I felt lifeless, afraid and unsure of myself.

I believe that in our lifetime we have soul lessons, and everything is happening *for us*. In the midst of this calamity and train wreck, it was difficult to see the gift, but since then I have shifted, grown, and created true inner peace. I'm now living the most abundant life.

Some may call this my dark night of the soul, my spiritual awakening, or upper-limiting. I call it my greatest gift.

I was forced to create change from a space of ill health. It's so common that we as entrepreneurs wait for an illness or a loss to realign our lives, but it doesn't have to be this way. You can be healthy and conscious, and notice when you feel resistance or out of alignment. This is your opportunity to listen in and receive the guidance to make a shift in your life.

From a brain perspective, I had moved into the unfamiliar. In the three months prior, I had invested $102K in coaches, a high-level mastermind, and a publicist. Hitting $100K in a week was a quantum leap but without the necessary support, understanding and psychology, I was unable to manage this shift.

"I just want to be back to normal," I said to my therapist. I was desperate to get back to my former self. I didn't realise that I was in survival mode. I had no boundaries, I was overworking, addicted to achieving, and making money to fill a deep void of not feeling good enough. I could feel my energy rise when clients had high cash months and then feel completely depleted when things didn't go to plan. Through therapy, my therapist helped me uncover that I had been dealing with anxiety since I was about 10 years old.

Going back to "normal" was neither an option nor a place that I should ever have wanted to go back to. We aren't meant to live in highs and lows, or to use drugs, sex or alcohol to numb ourselves from reality. True inner peace is just that: peaceful. We feel everything in a more divinely connected way, instead of the pull of drama, tantrums or busyness to avoid our truth. Without the emotional rollercoaster determined by your external world, you come back to yourself and your magnificence. At first, this can feel boring and too often we seek out drama, fighting with others, and old patterns to fulfill this need for an emotional adventure.

Burning out was my old identity. Of course, I wasn't meant to end my life, but this was my wake-up call. I needed to create better boundaries, let go of taking on responsibility for others, and stop overworking. I needed to be able to set up growth in my business in a consistent, sustainable and fulfilling way.

My ego loved the $100K sales week, but with the way my business was set up, I couldn't have created that consistently without burning out. I didn't have the team that was needed, the system, energy or mindset to hold space for that.

In these dark moments, I learned the power of faith, surrender and healing. Even while my brain was not functioning fully and I was terrified of having to go back to London and start a corporate job (that I would have hated), clients still continued to find me.

I was forced to take two weeks off to rest, heal, and continue to move forward with my business in a healthier, more sustainable way. The healers, therapists and coaches that I needed to support my journey continue to appear, and my healing journey continued.

The years after my crash, I was led to study and learn Reiki, NLP, shadow work, inner child healing, quantum healing, Human Design, and breathwork facilitation. It was a big year of learning! Having all of these teachings in my toolbox has made my work unique because I now focus on combining mindset, energetic embodiment, heartset and intuitive marketing in alignment with Human Design. It's everything I've learned to support you with being paid to be you.

Although my burnout was a traumatic experience, it redirected my life and guided me to inner peace, faith and purpose. Through this low point in my life, I'm able to have more blissful appreciation for the little things and don't feel like I need to do, buy or create something in order to *feel.*

You and I are infinitely guided and protected.

WHAT DO YOU WANT YOUR GRAVE STONE TO SAY?

For most of my life I was operating from a space of "the harder you work, the more money you make" and "you're only successful when you have material wealth."

I overworked, I spent a lot of time in a state of drama, constantly feeling overwhelmed and crying from frustration. I was riddled with anxiety, guilt and imposter syndrome. Although I would appear happy to the outside world (I was a master at pretending everything was fine), I didn't know what fun really was. When I was 34, I sat down and made a list of what would be fun for me, and started to incorporate more of this into my day. At first, it meant a meeting request saying "go have fun" but today, fun, pleasure and joy is infused into every day and everything I get to do. So much so that when Shaun and I were reflecting on 2020, he turned to me and said: "You know what has shifted so much this past year for you? You find joy in everything you do. Even when you're doing tasks in the business that you didn't enjoy, you find a way to create fun." It feels amazing to acknowledge how far I've come and how different life now looks.

Almost wanting to end my life made me stop taking life for granted. It helped me see that every day is a blessing. From the people to the opportunities you have, there is always something to be truly grateful for.

Stop for a moment, and think about your list of things you *have to do*.

Replace *I have to* with: *I get to.*

How different does it feel to move from I should, I must, and I have to, to, *I get to?*

"Vanessa, how would you feel if your gravestone said: *She made a lot of money and worked hard. She proved and tried to show everyone she is worthy.*"

Although I laughed when my therapist, Ellie, said this, the level of truth in that was frightening. If I continued the way I was, filling every second of every day with work, more than likely that's what it would be.

This felt better:

"Vanessa lived a life of fun, pleasure and joy. She left a legacy, transformed the lives of others, and she was a loving daughter, sister and partner. She lived life to the fullest, always experiencing adventures, and if you were ever in her presence you could feel the happiness of a life well lived."

Life is not about working hard and sacrificing other areas. It's not about making money and doing work you hate. It's about living fully and purposefully. It's about coming alive within, feeling vibrant, and being happy. Most of us have it all backwards, I certainly did. I so badly wanted to make money, weigh less on the scale, and buy things. I was so preoccupied with those things that I forgot to have fun and be happy. The moment I put happiness, fun and pleasure first in all areas of my life—from how I eat, move, dress and work—the work was done in a more powerful way. I raised my vibration and I started to attract more abundance in all areas of my life.

Let's take some action and make your dreams a reality:

Soul Reflection

- What does fun look like for me?
- If I were to allow more fun, pleasure and joy into my life, what would that look like?
- What would change in my life if you had more fun?
- What do I want my gravestone to say?
- What am I ignoring that feels out of alignment?

UNDERSTANDING WHY YOU SELF-SABOTAGE

When we are making huge shifts, moving through old patterns and creating a new reality, self-sabotage is common. The brain and body love the familiar. It's easier to stay the same than to change. The brain loves taking the path of least resistance, often telling us that change is unsafe and uncertain.

Self-sabotage is not always a flaw—oftentimes, it is a necessary tool to keep us safe. There is a light and a shadow side to it. If you're ready for a big uplevel, understanding what is happening is key.

We all have an invisible inner setting that determines how much money, success, love and abundance we will allow based on our programming and beliefs. This is your comfort zone. The minute we exceed that setting—by making more money, experiencing more love, and drawing more positive attention to ourselves—we get into an unfamiliar space. What we believe is possible and how we shift through these levels is dependent on our childhood conditioning, the evidence we have, and our understanding of the quantum realm.

As soon as we go beyond this point, a little voice inside us says, "You can't possibly feel this good." So, we find ways to bring ourselves back to the familiar. Most of the time this is completely unconscious. If you choose to create an awareness around your patterns of self-sabotage then you're able to shift them and uplevel with more ease. Outside of our comfort zone is our courage zone. This is the zone where we come alive and feel vibrant, excited and fulfilled. However, change takes action and energy. It takes shifting and letting go.

I have had moments when shifting my vibration and frequency where clients will fall out of programs, friends may no longer be aligned, a team member or a program needs to go. In order to make space for something new, we will often experience an old identity, something in our business, or people falling away. This is part of the process of evolution and growth. What I know to be true is that when I make a massive shift, the clients that remain also shift powerfully. This may feel uncomfortable and like we have little control. We'll feel like reverting back to old habits and patterns—but if we want change, we need to move through this space of discomfort so that those people and opportunities that are meant for us will come into our world.

I had a powerful conversation with my Reiki master, Colleen, before I did my Reiki Level 1 attunement. "If you want your old life, keep it," she said. "If you want to have the life you're meant to, let the past go, and let yourself be guided."

If I'm honest, I didn't really understand at the time what could be wrong with my life. I said to her, "I have an incredible business, I make money, I get to do what I want, and my relationship is great. Why would I change this?"

Of course, the way I was self-sabotaging was unconscious at the time. She made me aware of what I was holding on to, and where I was fighting for my current reality in fear of things falling apart. There was a pattern of things going wrong and once they got better, I would sacrifice something. The first time I was consciously aware of my pattern and how I self-sabotaged was after my first 6-figure launch of *Supercharge Your Success by Design*. I began feeling guilty and had this fear of not being able to deliver. I then took on too much responsibility for my clients and ate poorly, which ultimately affected my energy levels and my fear came true: I didn't show up fully.

The last time I repeated this pattern, Shaun and I had booked a weekend away at one of our favourite 5-star resorts in Uluwatu, Bali. It was absolute luxury and we were taken care of at *such* a high level. I had just had a successful launch with several new clients but the guilt was setting in. *Who am I to make this much money? Am I a fraud? Did I charge too much? How am I going to deliver on my promises?* I was on edge the whole weekend. I was checking in with clients and asking if they needed support. I had this fear that they would stop working with me. I was preoccupied with my business and didn't allow myself to rest, be present, and enjoy the moment. I ate until I felt sick, and tried to consume anything that was unhealthy. By the time I went back home, I was tired, and although I showed up, I didn't feel confident or vibrant. As expected, the next month was a lower month, perfectly aligned with how I was showing up in all areas of my life.

There have been many moments in my business where I felt I was flying high and achieving everything with ease. Clients were pouring in, I had more money saved than usual and life felt amazing. Within the same breath, I was doubting myself, I would pick a fight with Shaun, and I would start to overeat. I would go into masculine overdrive. I would then start to doubt that I could do it again and irrational fears would come up. *Maybe I'm not good at this. What if it never improves?*

Now I know that I don't have to feel a particular way to make money or get clients. I know that it is already taken care of.

I also don't make a lower money month mean anything, either. I create an awareness around what may have happened and what I would do differently, but I don't get fixated on one lower month. Sometimes in periods of big inner shifts, my income has been affected. It doesn't have to be this way, but if it does, it is not the end of the world. I'd rather focus on the impact that can be made, and continue to show up for my bigger vision. The next level is truly in not being affected by what is external to you and showing up as if whatever you want is done. We give so much power to things external— arguments with partners, a "bad" food day, someone not buying, a client not getting a huge shift that our ego wants. These are all things that we tend to give our attention to, to distract us from our truth.

Today, I've adopted a mantra that I use every time I am shifting through discomfort and my world feels like it is falling apart.

Life is allowed to get better and better.
How good will you let it get?

Expect miracles daily, expect shifts to happen, and expect your life to grow and expand in miraculous ways. Take intentional actions towards what you desire rather than making decisions and taking actions that lead you *away* from your bigger vision. When things don't work out how you thought they should, have compassion for the growth because it's leading you exactly where you need to go. It is always this or better.

SHIFTING YOUR IDENTITY

In order to shift your identity or break old habits, you'll need to shift the way you think and feel. It is common to feel anxious, have old trauma come up, and feel uncomfortable as we teeter on the edge of something new. This is *growth* and human beings are born to evolve and shift. The discomfort doesn't have to be present and we can move through it incredibly quickly. Remember that it is never just discomfort— you can also simultaneously be holding the excitement of what is to come. It is not contraction before expansion, it is contraction and expansion at the same time as we shift and are shaped for what is being

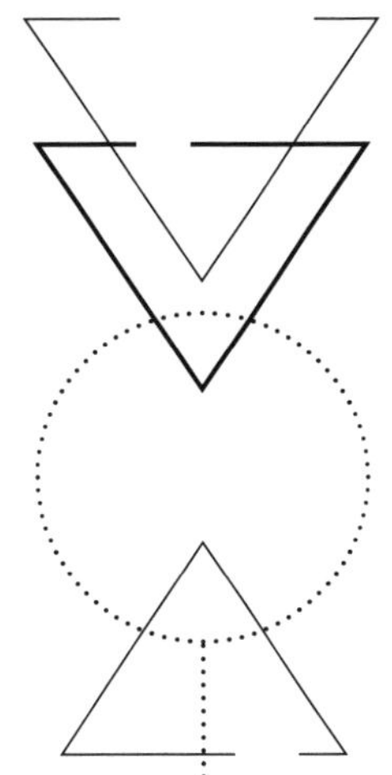

Life is allowed to get better and better. How good will you let it get?

revealed. Whatever is meant for you, is already in your energetic field. It already exists.

Why is my vision different to yours?

Why is my book not something you can write?

You are unique and that is your superpower.

HOW YOU CAN MANAGE THE SHIFT

1. Recognizing your self-sabotaging thoughts and patterns

When we are shifting our identity, it is common to start having thoughts like, "I'm too tired, I'll try tomorrow," or, "It's okay to feel bad, it's your dad's fault! Remember what he did?" On some level, it feels good to feel bad, especially if what we have had most of our lives is struggle, pain and unhappiness.

Remember to check in with yourself. Often clients I work with will go into pushing, controlling and masculine (doing) overdrive after feeling happy. Upleveling takes surrender (feminine) and trust that whatever is falling away will be replaced by something better as we continue to show up (masculine action) for our bigger vision. To surrender and have faith, we need to relinquish control. On the other hand, clients will disappear for weeks on end and sleep the days away telling themselves that they are tired, when really it's a way to avoid discomfort. Other times, rest is an essential part of the healing process.

Know thyself and recognise your habits and patterns. Without judgement.

Remember, you receive from the feminine, but to shift your being there is an action that is often required. That action may be taking a bubble bath or going to the spa, or it may mean showing up online and sharing the new program or a message that feels uncomfortable.

Get curious and ask yourself:

- If I was truly honouring myself, what would I need at this moment?
- Am I really tired, or am I avoiding something?
- If I stopped avoiding and showed up like the 7-figure version of myself, what actions would I take?

You can't make a wrong decision or move if you're making it from the soul. Every decision you make will lead you down a path you are meant to be on for your soul's growth.

2. Shifting your addiction to guilt, pain and suffering

"I'm only available for love and above." This is what a client said on one of my* Supercharge Your Success By Design *mastermind calls. She had held on to a lot of guilt and shame from past trauma and things that had happened in her childhood.

I've had so many examples of ruining moments that are meant to be pleasurable. I shared my experience in Singapore and the argument I had about the beautiful (and expensive) meal. There were so many other moments of being on holiday and arguing, overeating when I felt good, or pushing myself to exhaustion. I wouldn't allow myself to feel too good or too happy.

Now when I have these moments I ask myself: *how can I turn up this good feeling? What would that look like*? Become aware of how you self-sabotage, and then choose differently. That is all that is needed to shift this.

You may have an unconscious addiction to pain, guilt and struggling because these are the emotions that are most familiar. On some level, feeling bad is what is most familiar to us so when we start to feel happy, free and vibrant, we often self-sabotage to bring us back to what feels most familiar.

Many of my clients also feel various degrees of discomfort when money comes easily to them. They feel a sense of guilt, or feel that they've had "luck" when it comes easy to them but not to others—especially their clients. **We are meant to manifest with ease.** If this resonates with you, I doubt that life has been all ease and flow! You've just had an operating system wired for achievement and you've been totally unconscious of how you truly manifest things. Manifestation comes from the balance of ease and flow (feminine) and taking aligned action (masculine).

If you're used to feeling guilty, you'll self-sabotage to give yourself something to feel guilty about. Your body becomes addicted to that feeling of guilt. Trying to change that is like going through withdrawal—allow the discomfort, be aware of where you are self sabotaging, and allow yourself to choose differently in the moment.

Give yourself permission to free yourself from guilt. Allow yourself to expand what you think is possible for you, in turn, helping those around you do the same.

3. Honour and embrace fear and doubt

In these periods of shifting and moving past our old set point, it is common for irrational fears and doubts to surface. Most fears aren't real (unless there's a real threat to you)—it's just the brain trying to keep you safe. Reassure yourself, recognise what is happening, and allow yourself to choose a new empowering thought.

Get curious with what the fear and doubt is showing you. Often the fear is telling you that you're meant for this. The fear shows you that you are alive and it is worth it. Often fear and resistance is the subconscious reassuring you that big things are happening.

I used to have a repeated fear around losing the business and having to go back to a corporate job. The beginning of the month would start in a panic about where I'd get clients, despite having sold millions of dollars of programs online.

At this stage, I wasn't fully in my truth. I wasn't fully confident in what I was selling and a lot of what I was selling was work I had adapted from coaches I had worked with. When I wasn't using my unique gifts, signature methodology, and true belief, there was a real fear of things falling apart.

ENERGY LEAKS AS YOU UPLEVEL

It is important to look at *what the fear is showing you* instead of trying to avoid it altogether. In the above example, the fear was showing me that I needed to shift my program and connect to what I was really great at. It was guiding me to what I was meant to create in the world and to invite me to create a business that is sustainable.

▷ What is your fear showing you?

Allow yourself to sit with this question to unlock your next level of income and impact.

As you uplevel and shift, it is common to start seeing energy leaks and other things stopping you from moving to the next level of income and impact. We need to be aware of the signs instead of suppressing them.

An energy leak is when we're expending energy in ways that cause a decrease in our energy. For example, an energetic deficit is created by:

- Saying "yes" when we really want and need to say "no."
- Doing things because we're afraid that someone won't like us or love us if we don't.
- Receiving a comment or message from a client or someone in our community that is mean or triggering and having days of drama around it.
- Focusing energy on things that we can't change.

- Ex-partners or family members asking for something and us perpetuating the pattern.
- Hanging out with people that zap our energy just to please them.
- Holding on to anger.

I remember the first time I had a client drop out of my program. (I haven't had this for years now because of this awareness.) At the time, it was a huge deal for me. I blamed myself, I thought I was a terrible coach, and I wondered whether my program was good enough. It got me into a whirlwind of drama, berating and unworthiness. I wanted to be "perfect" and have everyone get huge shifts (my ego running the show). I was also operating from a fear of abandonment.

The next time it happened, I asked myself: *why is this happening for my growth and evolution? If this is showing me energy leaks and what I need to look at, what is it telling me? What is the lesson I need to learn?* It led me to creating firmer contracts in my business to ensure I was covered legally, made me get a lot stricter on who I take into the programs, and created a list of the non-negotiable attributes of the clients I work with. You get to choose who you work with. We are meant to feel energised, excited and grateful to work with the clients we have.

Now I know that the clients that come into my programs are ready for real change and they're committed to doing the work. It helped me raise my vibration and set up the foundation in my business for sustainable growth that is profitable, impactful and also feels great for me.

GETTING SICK OR INJURED

In over six years of running my business, I've never had to cancel a client or sales call without ample notice. It's not that I haven't been sick—but when I am, I know that it's likely a result of upper-limiting, self-sabotaging or a sign to slow down. I give myself compassion, rest, and choose to honour myself fully.

When things are going well, some of us have the pattern of getting sick or hurt. If you look back on the times that you have fallen ill or injured, ask yourself: did it come just after a big win in your business, a great time in your relationship, or when your body felt amazing?

Of course, not all illnesses or injuries are upper-limiting or self-sabotage, but it is important to understand that it *could* be. We often neglect looking at how the mind or emotions impact our physical health. Illness can also allow us to rid ourselves of stagnant energy and slow us down if we have been overdoing it. The more we start to listen to our bodies and rest where needed the more you can work with yourself instead of against your natural rhythm. So if it does happen, don't beat yourself up—have the rest, be with it, and you can get back to working on your business when you're ready.

Illness is also multi-layered—some clients only received attention and connection with their primary caregiver when they were sick or when their primary caregiver was sick. As humans, we will do anything for safety, connection and receiving love. When you stop receiving attention from this (not beneficial) what will you then connect over? It is important to understand that sometimes we benefit more from being ill than from wellbeing. Be mindful of the patterns. If you identify with this, see what else you can connect with that person on, and what positive way the relationship could shift.

PERFECTIONISM AND PROCRASTINATION

A lot of perfectionism tendencies are rooted in fear, insecurity and not feeling worthy. It can be an excuse to remain in your comfort zone. *I'm such a perfectionist, I won't get this out there until it is perfect.* I've heard that from clients a lot. When we understand that things aren't *good* or *bad,*we can start to explore the gift in everything, so we can learn how our patterns are currently hindering us.

Perfectionism usually starts as a way to get approval, love and attention from a deep wound of not feeling good enough. I often see clients who struggle with perfectionism, subconsciously still trying to receive the approval from a parent or loved one.

Understanding why you procrastinate and have a need to be perfect by an external standard is an important thing to look at. Consider the following questions:

- ▷ Where does my need to be perfect come from?
- ▷ What is the GIFT in my perfectionism? (Often it has allowed you to achieve and create to a really high standard. When you take away the energy and panic behind it, you can create in peace with far more pleasure.)
- ▷ What do I want to release?

  E.g. The panic of getting something done last-minute.

- ▷ What do I want to keep?

  E.g. Because of my programming, I always create amazing things.

STORING TRAUMA IN YOUR BRAIN

At 13, I started pulling out my hair when I was studying. I was deeply afraid of not getting good enough grades. When I burnt out in 2018, my therapist mentioned it was an anxiety disorder called Trichotillomania. I had high functioning anxiety from childhood trauma. Later in life, whenever I went to study, I would feel this same fear and response (although I had stopped pulling my hair out). I struggled to study for years and even focusing on reading a book was difficult for me. As you can imagine, this was a huge hindrance.

The triggers can be a particular sound, taste, feeling or sight. Trauma is stored in the brain and in the body. I used to get incredibly angry when I heard a drill or lawnmower. Living on a golf estate, days would often start with me being appalled at how early they were mowing the lawn. It was completely irrational and reactionary. I realised that when I burned out, they were drilling next door while building a new house and I was unable to sleep. It was also tied to childhood trauma with drilling.

In order to understand these trauma responses, we need to understand the amygdala's function. The amygdala is the brain's alarm system controlling the fight, flight or freeze response. It also stores all memories of previous situations which have created strongly negative emotions. When we are faced with anything the brain perceives as dangerous, the amygdala sends cortisol (the stress hormone) to close down higher brain functions of the prefrontal cortex and diverts energy to the back of the brain to prepare us for action in an emergency. In this state, there is less glucose and oxygen available for intellectual processing affecting memory, decision making, and creative ideas, and we tend to make more sweeping statements that are unjustified. The amygdala is also responsible for phobias.

The amygdala stores all negative memories and it is why childhood trauma and experiences have such a big impact on us, even if we don't remember the details of the event. The 'away from' approach of resisting change because it is seen as dangerous is more powerful than the 'going to' reward response. We will do anything to avoid that same response and pain.

Danger can mean symbolic danger, like doing a Facebook Live, launching a new program, or creating a course. It can also include hearing an opinion that we perceive as an attack or feeling belittled or misunderstood. You may experience an irrational fear and response, a reaction that bypasses your logical reasoning process. If this is the case, understand that there are processes to support you with shifting through this. You don't have to resign yourself to thinking that this is *just the way it is* or the way things are.

HEALING TRAUMA AND UNDERSTANDING YOUR HABITS

Growing up I had a lot of difficult moments, which turned into trauma and led to me developing survival-mode patterns. I was not honouring my basic needs, there was a lack of love, lack of attachment, and deep fear of people leaving me. Through sessions with my Reiki healer, I learned that because of all the trauma I'd experienced as a kid, I had to relearn who I was and give myself the love I didn't receive growing up.

So often we downplay what we've gone through. We tell ourselves that it *wasn't that bad,* or that it *could have been worse.* The truth is, we can only set ourselves free from these responses by acknowledging that trauma is trauma, no matter the scale. It is also a gift—it makes us who we are.

If we don't heal the underlying trauma, we end up acting and behaving from that wounded part of ourselves, often making decisions from the version of us where the trauma occurred. Yes, that may mean your seven-year-old self is running your business. Obviously, running your business and managing your team like an unloved seven-year-old is a recipe for disaster. The great news is, you can start to process and uncover how the trauma has impacted your habits, behaviours and beliefs *now.*

From severe trauma, you disenfranchise from a lot of your gifts and often disown parts of you. Those parts want to be seen, loved and integrated. It is important to call back all parts of you to feel fully whole. It's not easy work, but it's important.

Soul Reflection

- What was the trauma?
- How old was I?
- What did the trauma make me believe about my worthiness, loveability and enoughness?
- What parts of myself have I forgotten because of the trauma?

- What do I need to say to those parts of myself?
- What am I ready to call back and own now?

TRANSMUTING TRAUMA AND EXPANSION

When you're in a space of rapid expansion, upleveling, and an increase in abundance, pleasure and purpose, most people experience a trauma response. Often, this is tied in with receiving from their past where it doesn't feel safe, or because they don't feel capable of holding on to the expansion.

We often don't even know where the trauma is being held, because we're actually really good at working around blocks and accommodating them. It's like when you have shoulder pain, you will find a way to manage and work around it until it gets worse. It is why on many levels, it feels safer to contract when expansion shows up, which then creates resistance and keeps us in familiar patterns.

Resistance means we have to work harder for what we truly want. We are focusing more energy on what can go wrong or what won't work out than actually focusing on receiving and holding on to the expansion. As long as you're bracing for something bad to happen, you're not receiving at the level that you're meant to.

In order to receive and then hold onto what we receive, we must raise our vibration and transmute the trauma.

Transmuting Trauma So Expansion Can Take Place

Feel the fears, feel the sensations in your body, feel past trauma, past mistakes and things you are afraid of. So often we try to repress or shove them down. Observe everything in the body. If you need to cry, scream or shake your body do so. Ask yourself the following questions, and journal on them.

Journal prompts

- What are you really afraid of by expanding your business?
- Why is it not safe?
- What have you done/lost or faulted on in the past that you're afraid of repeating?
- What have you seen as a child when you had more money?
- What are you telling yourself you will lose if you expand?
- How are you protecting yourself from that wounding and at the same time, stopping expansion?

    E.g. Not showing up in the way that I want to, hiding out, not sharing what I want, focusing on everything that will go wrong.

- Why is it more safe for your business to expand?
- If it is safer, what do you need to release?

- What do you need to put in place now to support your expansion to cultivate safety?

  E.g. Structures for finances.

- If I was to transmute trauma into power and boldness and 6 figure launches were easy, effortless and divinely guided I would...

  I often redirect my energy by saying: "Vanessa, you can focus on the problem but what if you focused on the solution? How would you feel, think and act then?"

It is time to step up in a big way— it takes far more energy resisting your power and boldness than it is to flow, awaken to your desires and amplify your impact.

Awake your soul.

Awaken your pleasure.

Honour your desires.

Remember who you are.

It's time.

EMBODIMENT & NERVOUS SYSTEM

For most of my life, I was disconnected from my body and its natural cues. I didn't know what my body needed to feel nourished, safe or supported. I was even disconnected from basic needs like knowing when to rest, when to go to the toilet, when I was thirsty, or when I needed something to eat.

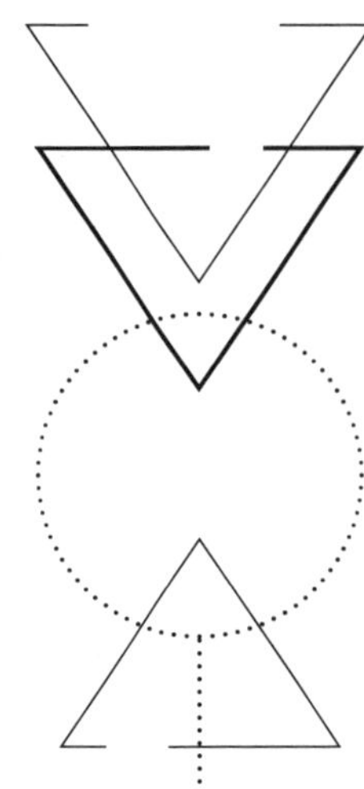

It is time to step up in a big way— it takes far more energy resisting your power and boldness than it is to flow, awaken to your desires and amplify your impact.

I was disconnected from my body and stuck in anxiety. I was afraid to feel, so I continued to push, prove and do more to avoid my trauma and truth. I was so afraid after burnout that I would go back to that scary place, that I tried to keep myself safe through self-sabotage and inactivity.

The other day, a client signed up to join *Supercharge Your Success by Design,* and one of the questions she asked before signing up was: "Will building my business affect my health? I am so afraid of going back to where I was when I was bedridden." She had thyroid and autoimmune disease and had healed significantly, but she was afraid of going backwards. The fear of that trauma was still stored in her body, so unconsciously, she had sabotaged her success to stay in a familiar space. She said she wanted to sign clients, but this clearly showed that it was not safe to do so. It was safer in her mind and body to be where she was, although she knew she was made for more.

An incredible thing about the work I do is supporting clients with healing their trauma. I have the tools and experience, and I've found a number of clients have felt more vibrant, alive and happy through speaking their truth, using their gifts, and doing the work they are meant to do. And interestingly enough, metaphysically, thyroid issues are associated with holding your tongue and not speaking your truth.

Do you often struggle to slow down, sit quietly, and take time for yourself? If you do, are you on edge and feeling guilty? This is a survival mode pattern, rooted in lack of attachment in early childhood.

This used to be me.

If you have had any kind of trauma, you may disassociate from the body, as it no longer feels a safe place to be. Through trauma you also may dissociate from your soul, which is called *soul loss.* This dissociation creates an overactive mind, which feels like *being stuck in the mind.* Often what happens is you become stuck in either high or low levels of dissociation or arousal, or swinging between these two states. The rollercoaster of highs and crashing lows has a negative impact on your nervous system.

When your nervous system has been conditioned to be in a state of hyperarousal (fight or flight) this can feel familiar, which means that slowing down and resting can feel unfamiliar and uncomfortable. Our bodies function best when they feel safe and loved. You can only take on as many clients as your nervous system allows. Your nervous system will protect you from taking on too much. It is why many people remain at a plateau after taking on a number of clients, or can also struggle to take on initial clients. The conscious brain will tell you that you want more clients and money, but the subconscious mind and nervous system will tell you it is not safe!

We must not confuse familiar with safe. They are not the same.

A common pattern with the women I work with is periods of pushing followed by exhaustion or burnout. You push through to the weekend, you push through the launch, and you live for your next holiday. *But resting isn't the same as regulating your nervous system.*

Regulation is teaching the nervous system and the body to feel safe and loved on a daily basis.

It is essential that it happens daily, otherwise we will see a decline in relationships, health and in our business.

After burnout (from years of hyperarousal) I would get outside in nature, do yoga, do journaling etc., but I was still afraid of slowing down and being present with myself. I felt stressed and anxious, scrolling through my phone, comparing myself to others, and afraid that my clients wouldn't get results.

I wasn't using the down time to teach my body to feel safe, calm and loved. I wasn't learning to keep my nervous system in balance either. This meant, as soon as I was busy again, attending to the other responsibilities of life, I was still the same person, operating with the same dysregulated nervous system... just a bit more "rested."

I was the same person. I wasn't changing, and it kept me in a perpetual state of exhaustion.

90% of communication comes from the body up to the brain and only 10% of communication happens from the brain downwards. This means that we repair the nervous system by creating self-awareness, connecting to the sensations of the body, and honouring them with love and care. **Not** by trying to use the brain to create routines that look good on paper, that we *have* to or *should* follow. It is why motivation alone or trying to push through doesn't create lasting change.

Repairing the nervous system occurs by taking the time to slow down, and cultivating a deep and loving connection to the felt sense of our everyday experiences.

To start to come back into your body:

- Lie on the floor, and do a body scan. What are the sensations you have in the body? Are there parts of your body that feel sore or stiff?
- Keep breathing into your belly and heart.
- Is there anything that your body needs? Ask your body: "Body, what do you need right now?"
- When you eat your next meal — observe how the body feels, how the food tastes and the textures that you notice.

Feeling and awareness is freeing.

3 THINGS TO DO TO REGULATE YOUR NERVOUS SYSTEM

1. SLOW DOWN: This doesn't mean stop completely. It means bringing more presence to what you are already doing each day. If you are walking on the beach or outside, take note of your surroundings and slow down to see the trees, the sun on your face, and listen to the sounds of the birds. Bring more presence and attention to your daily activities. When you're working on your business, slow down to be present, if you're eating, really taste your food.

2. TUNE IN: Think of your nervous system as a young child. It needs love and attention. We bring that love and attention to our nervous system by being attuned to our body. This means noticing what sensations and emotions are present and naming them without judgement or creating a story about what you notice. Whatever you notice, just name it without judgment. The more you understand your needs and attend to them, the more regulated your nervous system will become. E.g. *My body feels warm and tingly,* or *I feel sad today and my heart feels heavy.*

3. BREATHE: If you've had anxiety or fatigue, likely most of your breathing is from the chest. Managing your breath is the only way you can consciously control the autonomic nervous system. Most of us live busy and stressful lives, and we need to slow down and feel. Simply coming back to the breath when you feel stressed or anxious shifts your state and creates new neural pathways without taxing your body, e.g. Dancing or frantically moving around.

The next time you feel a surge of anxiety or feeling overwhelmed, simply close your eyes and take a deep heart and belly breathe in for the count of 4, hold for 4, and release for 8. See what shifts.

HOW TO NAVIGATE SELF-SABOTAGE

Understanding the brain's functions, your beliefs, your nervous system, and how you upper-limit, will help you recognise when you are getting out of your comfort zone and creating something new.

I know I am going to the next level of income and impact when my mind starts screaming at me, I start getting anxious, sweating, or have fear-thoughts. I know that old trauma is coming up to be healed. The discomfort is showing me that expansion is on the horizon!

1. Awareness

Recognise and identify that you are doing big things and that you are upper-limiting, and then allow yourself to create familiarity and safety in what is happening.

- ▷ Why is it not safe?

  E.g. Making more money means more family members will want my money.

  Making more means more work.

  I made terrible money decisions that impacted my family and I'm afraid of doing it again.

- ▷ Why is it safe?

  E.g. The more money I make, the more I have to give, I don't have to give anyone anything but I would love to support a family member.

- ▷ What needs to be released?

  E.g. The belief that it isn't safe for me to have more, not believing that abundance is my birthright.

2. Reparent your inner child

Send love to the parts of you that are afraid.

> E.g. "I know this is scary, but it is going to be even better than you can imagine. I love you and you're going to do amazing things. I know it feels uncomfortable now but this is simply old stuff rising to the surface. Your truth is..."

3. Celebrate and shift your belief

Shift the way you perceive this discomfort— this is truly exciting, and the faster you embrace the change, the quicker you can move past it. I truly believe that from this space, you can choose to quantum leap and shift without setbacks. Everything is based on your beliefs. If you think it will take a long time and will be uncomfortable, it likely will be.

Change the narrative: "Woohoo, this is growth! I love growth"

4. Create your own mantra

Create a mantra that aligns with you and where you are. Old trauma that you thought you have healed may arise again. See the patterns, observe the new level of awareness and then connect in. My favourite is:

"That is old stuff, we have processed that before. Life is allowed to get better and better, how good will you let it get?"

5. Breathe!

Take 4 deep breaths in, hold for 4, and release for 8. Beautiful belly breaths. You are safe. There is no emergency.

RITUAL TO TRANSMUTE THE DISCOMFORT AND UPLEVEL

- Close your eyes, take a deep breath, recognise and feel the sensation of your body. Feel into the discomfort. Where is it present in your body?

- What is coming up for you to heal and feel?
- Whose fear and energy is here? Is it all yours or someone else's?
- What other emotions are present?
- What are your emotions guiding you to feel and heal?
- What is the next aligned action you are guided to take?
- Connect into *why* you want more. (I simply remind myself that I won't be at this level my whole life, I might as well take the leap now.)

Don't try to fix it, make it go away, or judge it. Be with this feeling. You have the capacity to hold all of the emotions of fear, excitement and discomfort. This is being alive. Don't fight or judge—simply feel and honour.

YOUR COMFORT & COURAGE ZONE

The comfort zone is just that: comfortable. It is your dead zone and it is where you tend to feel stuck, confused about the next step, and stay in a stagnant state. You may go around in circles with decisions because of the fear of the unknown.

I often hear things like: "If I change this will it actually get better? What if I make the wrong decision and I end up worse off?"

We so often make decisions from scarcity, or fear of it not working out.

Let's go there. Go to the worst case scenario. Maybe you hire a new team member and it doesn't work out, or you quit your job and you don't make enough money in your business. The worst case is no worse than the scenario you currently have, so you might as well take the leap, put what you can in place to create a smooth transition, and go for it.

Your comfort zone naturally expands with experience. The more you take small actions every day outside of your comfort zone, the more familiar you become. The compound effect is true! The small action with newfound faith builds over time to big courageous acts. When you have a high degree of faith that when you leap the net will appear to catch you, you start to genuinely feel that change and growth is exciting. This is where you are available for a big uplevel! Know that your map of the world and your propensity for change determines the actions that you are willing to take. This will differ from person to person.

Soul Reflection

- What action is just outside of my comfort zone that I can commit to?
- What would faith do?
- If I fully honoured and trusted that I couldn't make the wrong decision, what would I decide today?
- If I had $10 million in the bank, what would I do differently in life and business?
- From the list above, what can I implement now?

Start small and make it something you know you can commit to, so you can start to build up faith. Don't commit to a 5 a.m. workout when you know you prefer to wake up later. If you already have a high degree of faith and core routines, expand that—play with going even bigger.

Small forward actions taken in faith lead to giant leaps.

The courage zone is the space where we come alive but we don't know what is on the other side. It is unfamiliar, so the brain will try to keep us safe. This is the zone where possibility is endless and we are able to create whatever we desire. Tapping into flow and the realm of infinite possibilities.

Remember: when nothing is certain, anything is possible.

There are common patterns to be mindful of when you're uplevelling or moving into a space of growth. Be aware of them! When they come up, I say: "Oh, I'm changing! How exciting!" Be with them, see them for what they are, but know that this is simply helping you to adjust to what you are meant for. Avoid going back to old patterns.

- Your confidence may drop, and you may feel like you don't know enough.
- The things, people, and activities you used to enjoy may not seem as pleasurable.
- Everything may feel like it is falling apart, but the crumble of the old is necessary (trust it is all coming together, as it is meant to).
- You may begin to question yourself and your goals, such as thinking "maybe I don't need that much money," or "maybe I don't need to have a virtual assistant."
- You may feel alone, or like you no longer relate to others, even your close friends. You may feel numb to what used to inspire you.
- You may see failed payments, clients leaving you, or your team no longer being aligned. It is simply making space for the new.

All of these events are a chance to look deeper and see how whatever is showing up is moving you towards your bigger vision.

▷ **What is the growth opportunity I'm being presented with?**

When you are shifting you may be presented with energy leaks that you have. When you plug these and understand them, you are being given the pathway to your next level.

Perhaps you need to sort out your contracts, get firmer boundaries in place, or inform potential clients of the deadline for payment.

▷ **Do I have everything I need right now?**

Recognise that this is simply making space for more aligned clients. Remember when your vibration increases, those that aren't ready to be at that new frequency will potentially fall away but the clients that are ready will rise up massively.

- You may feel disconnected from your partner.

  Communicate and let them know how you feel. If you need more time to yourself or don't feel like doing the usual activities, communicate this with them. I would suggest not making any rash decisions at this time about your relationship. This shift is only temporary.

- Countless opportunities present themselves to distract you from your truth and from the discomfort. Shiny object syndrome is very prevalent.

  You may need to adjust. What got you *here* won't get you *there.*

  The systems, teams, boundaries and hours you work may need to shift. Connect in with what you want and adjust accordingly.

Journal Prompts

- How do you self-sabotage?
- Identify a time that you may have experienced an "upper-limit." What happened? Is there anything you could do differently if faced with a similar situation?
- How do you desire to navigate change and uplevelling?

Get Out Of Your Comfort Zone

My name is Leanna and I always loved the idea of having my own successful business, but in 2013, a series of unfortunate events (my husband lost both of his parents, our fourth baby was only 3 months old, we had a lot of financial trouble, and I was in a car accident left with a bad concussion) made me feel it wasn't safe to do so. Who was I to be able to breathe something all my own and share it without the world?

Through this time, I supported my husband, David, emotionally and mentally while he successfully opened his first physical therapy clinic. I was happy to support him in his dream. But what about me?

I turned to direct sales and found a community there. I found support "sisters" and successfully ranked in the top 2% of both companies. Even so, I knew deep down that my dream of opening my own business was still there, and the desire was growing again.

Vanessa showed up in my path at the perfect time (even though I didn't know it was the perfect time).

I was scared to jump all in, to acknowledge that I deserved to be paid as me, to be accountable to her guidance, and to allow that dream to come into full view.

A few months into our coaching, I started to see and feel the shifts. My desire had been all along to start my own business, and it was really happening authentically. I didn't need to be selling a product that wasn't mine! I was inherently enough to sell my coaching! What a phenomenal realization.

She energetically supported me through the entire process of creating *Huntress Coaching,* and I put all my selling energy into that. I realised it was inside me all along to dream big, to go big, and to make big money! My dream came into full view and it was beautiful!

One month into officially launching *Huntress* and I almost exceeded my highest year paid in a direct sales company! I have fulfilled my dream of being paid to travel to support a client with her mindset in a 3-day intensive.

I needed Vanessa and her guidance, her energy, her expertise and her support. My first program, *Intuitively You* wouldn't have been possible without her.

Reach out and schedule a call! That's what I did, and it changed my life.

LEANNA HUNT, Life Coach
www.huntresscoaching.com

chapter 6

Reprogramming Your Subconscious For Success

For a long time, I was a victim of my thoughts. Life was predominantly happening *to* me and I was at the mercy of my circumstances, childhood and trauma. I hated my body, I hated my corporate job, and I hated where we lived. It wasn't until I started to go deeper into studying the brain and the subconscious mind that I realised we truly have the power to shift our thoughts and reprogram our mind. We get to consciously create our reality and speak to our subconscious and ego in a "language" it can understand.

In a world filled with affirmations and an obsession with vision boards, there are more people than ever depressed (stuck in the past) and anxious (obsessed with and fearing the future). When there is dissonance between your subconscious and conscious mind, that is where feeling stuck comes from. We manifest from the subconscious, so until you are fully aligned with what you want to manifest and actually believe it is possible for you, affirmations and vision boards can actually be less motivating or useless. When your subconscious is on board (no pun intended) with those visions—that is where these tools create powerful shifts.

I've never had a vision board, yet I've manifested a life beyond what I could have ever imagined. It is never about what you do, it is about aligning your inner world so that your outer reality mirrors what you want.

Change one belief and thought, change your life.

This chapter is about understanding how to close the gap between your conscious and subconscious. It's about learning to work *with* your fears, resistance and doubts.

"If you are depressed you are living in the past.

If you are anxious you are living in the future.

If you are at peace you are living in the present."

— LAO TZU

When we are consciously aware of the thought pattern or the fear that is holding us back, we are either changing or choosing it. This is amazing, because we do have the power to shift our thoughts! However, the negative or positive benefit of letting that belief go may not be worth it. In other words, if you're stuck and not changing, it's because on some level, you're benefiting. It is why we need to understand the positive payoff someone is receiving from not changing.

The benefit of staying where you are is often rooted in perceived safety. Perhaps your parents will accept you more if you stay in your corporate job. Maybe your partner fell in love with the version of you that you're scared to leave behind. The list is endless, but understanding that it's normal and totally valid to want to stay where you are is crucial to having the courage to be able to change. We aren't meant to be stagnant. What needs to leave will leave, and the future will bring more excitement than you can even imagine... but it takes stepping into the courage zone.

We need to be present and grateful for what we have while simultaneously creating our new reality with faith that it *will* happen.

First, we need to understand how to speak to the subconscious mind, which runs 97% or more of what is going on in our reality. Often, when I first speak to clients, they have a belief that they can't manifest unless they are energized, excited, and Facebook Live ready. In other words: they believe they have to be experiencing "good" emotions to manifest. They suppress and shove down any negative thought patterns, in turn creating more dissonance and never truly moving forward. When we move from the berater that doesn't allow the negative thoughts or beats themselves up, to the observer, where you understand your habits and patterns and recognise that you are in the driver's seat, this is where change occurs. Whenever I see one of my old patterns, I'll laugh it off and say: "There's that pattern again, let's do something else instead, Vanessa!"

Your beliefs drive your behavior.

It doesn't matter how much you say you want something, if you believe deep inside that having what you want equals some kind of pain, then you'll get in your way and it won't happen. The great news is, you can reprogram your subconscious and get it on board with your goals.

HOW TO REPROGRAM YOUR SUBCONSCIOUS MIND FOR SUCCESS

We had been trying to manifest our dream house but it wasn't showing up as quickly as I wanted it to. I was clear on what I wanted and the investment we wanted to make, but it wasn't showing up.

I got curious and asked myself why it wasn't safe for me to have that house. Truth was, I was afraid on **so many levels** to buy a house. We had been moving around for almost 12 years (London and Bali) and making a commitment to stay somewhere and really settle down was terrifying. What if we didn't like it? What if the political and economic situation worsened in South Africa? In the estate we wanted to purchase the home, I feared it may not be easy to sell. What if we couldn't keep up the payments? The home I wanted was big and luxurious, and subconsciously I was scared of what my family would think. I heard my mother's voice calling a wealthy woman a "rich bitch."

The list went on. As you can see, it wasn't safe for me. It was "safer" to stay where we were, in a beautiful home with low commitments. But, it was not what I truly wanted. I wanted to experience our first home that was truly ours. I wrote everything out, walked to the estate where we wanted to buy, and said: "This is home, I am ready to live here for years to come. I am done living all over the world. I'm ready to find my dream home."

And I let it go, allowing the Universe to delight and surprise me.

Two days later, I was looking on the website for the places for sale in this estate. I said to myself: "Today I'm going to see my dream home," and guess what? There it was, even more perfect than I could have ever imagined.

As much as you want something, it may be *less safe* to have it. On some level, your subconscious will be protecting you from receiving it. When you are able to acknowledge and understand what it is, you are able to shift that belief.

7 STEPS TO REPROGRAM YOUR SUBCONSCIOUS MIND

Take out your journal and get curious with your subconscious. Don't overthink it, let your hand write whatever is coming through. The aim is to get out of logical thinking and into your subconscious thought patterns.

1. Recognise the Wisdom In the Resistance

When you think about your goal, what resistance do you have to it? Why is it not safe to manifest that desire? How are you positively benefiting from staying where you are?

Resistance can unlock a powerful gift. What is the resistance showing me? If I release it, what will happen?

2. Speak to Your Subconscious and Get Curious

You can speak to your subconscious like someone you're interviewing.

"Hey subconscious, what are you really afraid of? Having what you want is amazing but what does having that goal mean in your life? What is the sacrifice that you think you need to make?"

What is your subconscious trying to protect you from?

Why is it more safe to have what you want?

Get quiet, and listen to what that inner voice is telling you. Let it make its case. There's priceless wisdom in your fear. It's reminding you what matters most to you and what you truly want.

Remember you can have a conversation with your subconscious and ego at any time. Become great friends with your mind instead of at war with it. I like to speak to my inner child as well.

"I understand you're doing big things and this feels unsafe, but we've gone through it and we know that it is more safe to have what you want."

3. Commit to Making it Work

Now that you know what matters most, commit to looking out for it. Commit to creating it without sacrifice.

Let your subconscious know you got the message by promising it that you'll make it work. Promise you won't go after any version of success that means you'll lose what matters to you. You'll only go for it in a way that'll feel right for you and stay in alignment with your values. This is a really great step, because it stops making your fears an issue.

Those things you're afraid of? They're not inevitable. When you understand them, you can set yourself up for what you truly want. Making this promise lets your subconscious mind embrace your dreams and create space for you to pursue them. The promise means you've listened to your inner wisdom and you're honoring what's truly important to you, so you can let go of the fears that are holding you back.

4. Gather Positive Evidence

No doubt, you'll have tons of evidence to support your negative thought patterns. "If I make millions then I'll never have a life," or "I'll never have a launch that feels fun." Likely, your reticular activating system (RAS) is finding all the evidence to support your limiting belief.

Now, I want you to look at all the evidence that you can have *exactly what you want.*

E.g. There are a lot of millionaires that have more time and greater impact because they outsource, and can work exclusively in their zone of genius.

5. Remind Your Mind

Ongoing repetition is important to embed your new beliefs into your subconscious. These new belief repetitions are commonly called *affirmations,* but are simply reminders of what you know to be true. You shouldn't have to "fake it" or convince the mind. At this stage, they will feel like second nature to you.

Give yourself affirmations or mantras to remind your subconscious of the promise you've made. These are affirmations I truly believe in and they make sense to me. Create some of your own. My favourite mantras are:

"The more fun I have and the more I honour myself, the more money I make."

"I am a conscious creator, I get to have whatever I desire."

"If I can dream it, I can create it. That version of me already exists in the infinite field of possibility."

"Life is allowed to get better and better. That's just the way it is for me"

"The more money I make, the more impact I make and freedom I have."

Your mantra should include whatever messages you need to remember. Maybe you need to remind your subconscious that success will help you increase your time with your family or your freedom to travel, or that you have the power to resist busyness or the pressure of other people's expectations.

Repeat your mantra as often as it feels good to you, but especially at times when you have the most access to your subconscious mind. The best time to repeat your mantras is first thing in the morning, after meditation, or right before bed.

6. The Attitude of Gratitude

Having a daily practice of repeating your affirmations and connecting to what you are grateful for on a daily basis refocuses your attention on what you want. The more gratitude you have for the present, the more you can receive.

Being grateful helps us stay in the present and refocus our RAS on what we do want. The more it focuses on the positive, the more positive things will come into our reality.

7. Aligned Action

Now it is time to take action as if what you want is *already in your reality*. If you already had the house you wanted, what action would you take? If you already had a 6-figure launch, what action would that version of you take?

With a lot of mindfulness work, rewiring my subconscious, and managing my worry, I ended up rewiring and healing my brain. I was able to create new pathways and change the way my brain functioned. Neuroplasticity, in positive psychology, has shown that aspects of the brain can be altered, that it isn't fixed, and neuron damage later in life can be reversed. Stress, negative thought patterns, worry and trauma can have a profound negative effect on the brain.

The good news is, you can rewire your brain. You can change your neural pathways.

After burning out and being in a negative space, it took time to shift from scarcity and fear to abundance and faith. At this stage, I was afraid of losing the business, I was scared that I would continue to be negative and not be able to focus. I was afraid of everything: driving, being alone, and going to a public toilet by myself. There were two actions that I took in faith when I was incredibly afraid, that shifted me profoundly.

1. I gave to someone less fortunate: I now know that I am meant to be rich, and part of that is being able to give back freely and help others. I remember a cleaner that was working in a home we were renting. She was amazing and went over and above to look after us. I asked her what she really wanted to do with her life and she said that she wanted to be a Beauty Therapist. A couple of days later, just as we were about to leave, I paid for her tuition to study further. Just by giving, it was a shift from feeling like I don't have enough money, to feeling like there is more than enough, and I am overflowing. That was a powerful message for me. By giving, I said to the Universe: "There is always more than enough to save, invest, pay my expenses, and give back freely."
2. I did a Facebook Live: I had done numerous Facebook Lives before this one, but the confidence I once had felt like it was lost. Fears of not being good enough or saying something wrong were constantly coming up. I decided to look at those fears, embrace them, and do it anyway! I still remember how empowering it felt to finally do something I had put off for a few months.

Don't underestimate the power of taking small aligned steps just outside of your comfort zone. Faith, pleasure and action allow miracles to happen.

TRAUMA AND REWIRING THE SUBCONSCIOUS

If the subconscious belief is linked to deep trauma that feels incredibly uncomfortable in your body when you think about it, I would suggest using the Rapid Energetic Recoding™ method that can be found here ***www.vanessahallick.com/paid***. This method is taught within the Paid To Be You Certification. It is a rapid method of therapy combining several different techniques to resolve fears, phobias, anxiety, weight loss, smoking, and even PTSD. It is content free, so you don't have to rehash the past. I have used this for my fear of studying and pulling my hair out as well as my irrational fear of the sound of drilling which caused an outburst of anger. You can use this technique for as many days as you feel to truly shift your subconscious and release the body's response to trauma.

Take Charge Of Your Life

My name is Jess, and I am the founder and CEO of Empowered & True. My mission is to help people love themselves unconditionally and unapologetically so they can step into their truth and live the life they want to live. In early 2021, I had a vision for my business but I was building it slowly, as I was working in a firm at the time. After a new system was put in place in my film job (one of which went way past my boundaries), I thought I was going to be sick and I decided to go full steam ahead in my business. Through techniques like Breathwork and helping people turn inwards into themselves, I am able to help transform people's lives in the best way possible. Going all in with my business has been the scariest and most challenging time of my life, however, it is so worth it. I receive fulfilment and that is something I will strive every day to receive.

What stopped you from believing you could be paid to be you?

The main thing that stopped me from being paid to be me was time and space. The film industry is all-consuming. I had a passion for being a part of the film process but it didn't give me the fulfilment that my business gives me. Now that I have taken a step back from film, I am able to have the time, space and energy to fully invest into my business.

What was the shift that took place that led you to get paid to be you? How did it happen?

The shift that took place for me was when a new system was put in place on my film production that I didn't align with, and it made me extremely uncomfortable. I then realised that I wasn't financially stable enough to be able to walk out the door and not come back. This is when I decided to take charge of my own finances and future. I no longer wanted to rely on someone else to be able to support myself. I made the choice to take control of my life and build my business so if I were ever to be put in that position again, I would have the stability to be able to walk away.

What has your experience been working with Vanessa?

Vanessa is incredible! She is there to support you, to help you grow and also to call you out on your own bullshit. She has been one of my biggest supporters and her programs are extremely powerful. I would highly recommend Vanessa's programs to anyone wanting to grow as a person, do business on their own terms and to find out what they came here for. The Supercharge community that Vanessa continues to create has been such an incredible space to be a part of.

JESS ROWE, Self Love & Body Image Coach
www.empoweredandtrue.com

chapter 7

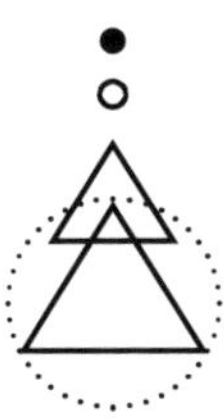

Money Mindset & Being Paid

After burning out, I was afraid of losing the business and having to return to a corporate job. I was living in a scarcity mindset around money. I had to let go of my obsession around making money to feel successful and the deep fear I had around losing it or being broke.

Money fears and stories run deep and left unattended, they can rule your business and create a lot of unnecessary stress and worry.

If you take the stress and worry out of making money, you would simply make money!

It seems that simple because it is.

Now, money flows to me with ease, multiple 6-figure launches are my reality, and I make millions online doing my soul work. You can transform the way you view money and create money.

I believe that money is all around us, like the air we breathe. It is in ample supply. It is not the hardest working or even the most knowledgeable that are rich—money is energy. Those that have an overflow of money have great wealth consciousness and a belief and expectation that it shows up in ample supply. You get to decide how money will show up for you.

You will never enjoy money if you're stuck in any of the following mindsets:

- Scarcity around money
- Fear of losing money
- Doing things for money that don't feel aligned
- Obsession with making money to feel worthy
- Linking your success and lovability to how much you make

My hope is that this chapter will help you heal your relationship with it and see the magic of money.

BEING PAID VS. BEING PAID TO BE YOU

Money is a vibration and frequency, and it comes from expecting, with faith, that it will show up. It is not about how healed, evolved or happy you are. I've made multiple 6-figures while anxious, unconscious and working long days. I believed that to make money I had to work hard and the harder I worked, the more I would make. The problem with being stuck in this paradigm is that we believe we have to work *even harder* to grow. Most of the clients I start to work with already feel maxed out and taking on more clients or increasing their income feels like it will only require more—more of them, more sacrifice, and more work.

The clients who I have worked with and who have committed to healing their relationships with money make a lot more money in less time, with more freedom, joy and pleasure. I know what I would rather choose!

I now believe that making money is easy, that I am divinely compensated, and the more money I make, the more impact I can make in the world. Good people making a lot of money can truly do great things.

You don't have to feel happy to make money, but this book is written to illuminate that you can have it all (and a ton of money) without sacrifice. One of my favourite mantras is: "The more fun I have and the more I honour myself, the more money I make." Having fun and pleasure in and out of my business has been a beautiful practice and choice I make on a daily basis. Even in the mundane tasks that I don't want to do, I find bliss or create it in some way. When you are your personal brand and your work focuses on supporting the transformations of others, it is *essential* to have fun.

This is the difference between *getting paid* and *getting paid to be you*. When you are paid to be you, you feel incredible, receiving money for your services feels amazing, you no longer fear losing it, you know that clients are in ample supply, and you trust that you'll be divinely compensated for your unique gifts.

The transition from being paid and being paid to be me came after burning out. Even at my lowest, money continued to flow and new clients arrived, but I was forced to do business differently. I went deeper into my money stories, I looked at my shadow self so that I stopped attracting clients that triggered me. I addressed my energy and focused on raising my vibration and frequency. I created, launched, and sold my signature programs in a way that felt aligned and fun for me.

MONEY AS A LOVING RELATIONSHIP

How do you speak to money? What do you currently believe about money?

If you keep telling your friend or partner that they are never around when they need you, more than likely, they won't want to be around you and will stop coming around altogether.

You need to start viewing money as a friend or intimate relationship.

Instead, start saying:

I love how you support me and are always there when I need you.

It's amazing how much our relationship expands and grows.

When I returned to my corporate job and had little money, instead of saying, "I would love to but I can't afford it," I would say, "I would love to but it's not a priority right now." And if it was a priority, I would find the resources. We can always find money when we get resourceful! It is in infinite supply.

At one point in my life, paying bills and going to the checkout scared me. I felt anxious and nervous. Today, every time I pull out my card to pay for something I'll say, "I'm so grateful I get to pay for this! Thank you Universe for my great abundance."

HEAL YOUR MONEY STORIES

The core function of the conscious brain is to distort, delete and generalise so that we can make sense of the world around us. Our memory is based on disconnected puzzle pieces which results in creating a current reality that isn't really your truth. Unless we create a conscious awareness of our thoughts, beliefs and actions, we continue to live a version of the past—past habits, beliefs and actions.

In my childhood, I had seen periods of "feast," where something on the farm was sold or we sold a piece of land. We would have a holiday, gifts, or eat out. It was always followed by "famine," when we hardly had money to pay for food. It created a real fear of money. I was scared of not having enough—of losing it all—and my insatiable drive to make money created a lot of stress and exhaustion. Financial trauma shows up in our businesses, and without creating an awareness and healing the relationship, we will forever feel like there is not enough.

I believed that:

"It takes hard work to make a lot of money."

"Rich people are greedy."

"Money doesn't grow on trees."

"You have to save for a rainy day—what goes up will go down."

▷ **Do any of these sound familiar to you? What beliefs do you hold about money?**

Your money stories are developed in the first eight years of your life. How you view money is therefore a distorted view of the truth around money, but it does tend to drive the show unless we are aware of it.

If money isn't showing up at the level you desire, on some level it may not be safe to do so.

▷ Why is it not safe to receive more?

Needless to say, I had a love-hate relationship with money. On one hand, success meant making a lot of money. On the other hand, my mom used to call rich people "rich bitches" and those that travelled business class "had more money than sense." I believed that making a lot of money was reserved for "others" and if you were rich, then you were a bitch. It created so much confusion around money. Since I didn't have a role model for wealth, I would go to the extremes of wanting a lot of material items, being overly obsessed with them, then feeling extreme guilt over wanting to be wealthy.

If we create separation or judge others for having money (or anything that we don't have for that matter), we create separation and push what we want further away. It is only our fear and our limited way of thinking that makes money seem scarce.

The opposite of fear is love. Fear can't exist in a space of love.

MONEY IS NEITHER GOOD NOR BAD

Money is in infinite supply. It's energy. It's all around us like the air we breathe. Money is neither good nor bad. It is neutral. The only thing that makes it good or bad is our perception of it.

When we shift our thoughts, words, energy and actions into alignment with the reality we truly want, we can't help but receive it. The faster you are able to shift into that new frequency with faith, is where you have the potential to collapse timelines: if you can see it in your mind, you can create it in reality. Whenever a client mentions their big goal, I always respond with: "It's already done." They laugh at me, but it's true! Whatever you want and the life that you are meant for *already exists.* If it is soul aligned and meant for you, it has already been done in the quantum realm.

Change your thoughts, beliefs and feelings and show up in faith that it is done. Keep showing up; don't stop. What you seek is seeking you! But we can't create a different reality while still being stuck in an old paradigm. Remember that you are a powerful creator. This means, you can shift your beliefs around money and how you want money to work for you and support you. When you have a powerful intention, you can create anything.

I believe that soul clients show up and love to pay me. In reality, clients are in fact excited to pay me! I believe that money flows in, grows and expands. I always have more than enough to save, invest, spend and pay all of my expenses with ease. I believe that making money is easy. I believe that it is safe to release large sums of money as I know that it returns to me in even larger amounts.

I trust money. Love is money and money is love.

When I understood the patterns and released the guilt, things started to increase rapidly and I was able to receive more than before.

These questions are what I asked myself in order to shift my reality. Grab a pen and paper, and really dig into the following:

- ▷ How do you want money to work for you?
- ▷ What is my new energetic minimum? What is the non negotiable I am available for in savings? What investments do I want to make?
- ▷ Why is it not safe to have this?

I had made a large investment in a coach right before burning out. I had a powerful realization that I associated the decision to invest money to being in a crisis, trying to find something/someone to blame. I created the belief that I am terrible with money and I can't be trusted, I believed that the more money I make the more money I waste.

- ▷ When we are holding on to something, there is always a positive payoff, even if it isn't desirable. How are you positively benefiting?

If I released the guilt, then I would have had to take ownership and responsibility for my actions. I was positively benefiting because it helped me stay safe and small (protecting me) to hold on to that guilt and it also stopped me from making other investments. At the same time, it was compounded with a fear around clients paying me, because I didn't want them to experience what I did, and think they had made a "bad investment" with me. This subconsciously kept me safe. Consciously, I wanted more clients, but just after burning out my nervous system was shot and I was afraid of taking on more clients. From this perspective, it was easier to blame the program and coach I was working with, than face the fact that I am responsible for my results and decisions.

▷ **How can you create this payoff in a positive way?**

I put in place a process when investing large amounts of money. I started to make decisions from an empowered place. The $60K investment was from ego and it wasn't based on hiring the person because they were the one I wanted to work with, but more based on how they had supported someone else to create results. She was the more expensive option, so I thought she must be better. I now know that everything happens *for* me and I can't make a bad decision with money. It is only bad if I make it so and continue to harbour guilt.

▷ **Why is it safe to receive large amounts of money?**

The more money I make, the more impact I make in the world, and the more I can give back freely to charitable causes.

Money is fun to receive, play with, and it creates more freedom

I make powerful decisions from a space of truth rather than scarcity. I now know how to make the decisions based on my human design. As a Manifesting Generator with an emotional authority, I need to wait to respond, receive a sacral response and then wait 24 hours to allow myself to ride the wave of emotions.

▷ **If I want to create consistent revenue I would...**

Often, clients say they want consistent revenue but their business systems, structures and offers are not aligned to consistency. If you want consistency in your business you need to set it up in this way. If you're going from bust to burn, look at where the gaps are. What would the multiple 7-figure version of you have in place for consistency? Think about your team, automation and your programs. What needs to shift?

ALLOWING YOURSELF TO RECEIVE MONEY

When I first started my business, I thought that receiving money from others meant taking from them, and that working with me would be a financial sacrifice. I was afraid to discuss money and the investment as well as go through the fears that they may have around money. Too often we shy away from this conversation with potential clients when, in fact, it is the most loving thing to do. There aren't enough honest and open conversations held around money. Journeying through fears around money and where the fears come from is powerful to unlock the scarcity mind to recognise infinite possibilities exist. When we live from scarcity or make decisions based on our current (or past) financial situation, we perpetuate the cycle and continue to stay in our current reality.

Often, we learn that receiving requires us to give something back. If someone gives to you, you may find yourself wondering what they want in return. Chances are, you have the same feelings around money. You may feel that to receive it would mean you "owe" something.

I remember a client who was undercharging and not making what she was meant to in her business. She was doing *so many* swaps. She'd get a facial and swap it for a coaching session. She'd do the same with her personal trainer. The issue with this is that she was never fully receiving. Allow yourself to receive the facial, allow yourself to receive support, and allow yourself to receive the activation in reading this book.

When you are having sex, think about fully receiving the pleasure. "I willingly and lovingly receive pleasure."

PAID TO BE YOU RITUAL

Close your eyes and take your left hand (feminine side of body) and tap on your heart seven times. Say the following out loud as you tap:

I receive the love

I receive the support

I receive the pleasure

I receive the money

I receive the joy

I receive the beauty

I receive the activation

Every time you receive money or find money, no matter how big or small, celebrate it. "Thank you, thank you, I love money."

CHARGING FOR YOUR SERVICES & BEING DIVINELY COMPENSATED FOR YOUR GIFTS

Often when clients start working with me, they are undercharging and undervaluing their services. Through mindset, energy and strategy work, things shift quickly.

Have you ever heard of *charging your worth* for programs? Well, you are priceless so that isn't very helpful. What gets mixed up is clients thinking they are the program, instead of the program being a separate entity. Yes, you are the guide and you deliver the program, but your worthiness is not linked to your clients success. You are worthy as you live and breathe.

Instead, consider the following questions:

- How will your clients feel when they complete the program?
- What are the tangible outcomes of the program if your client takes the aligned action?
- What is the lifetime transformation worth of the particular module or session?

When I work with clients, I do a two-hour intensive to uncover their unique gifts, signature methodology and messaging. Often our greatest and most powerful gifts are in what we are not sharing or have been disenfranchised because of trauma. We need to activate our innate gifts and remember the skills, knowledge and experience we have. There are no coincidences in what you have done and experienced up until this point in life. Your mess, journey, and what you have gone through makes you unique, and there is no such thing as *competition*. When you fully understand this, your confidence can soar and client results become more powerful.

You are meant to be divinely compensated for your natural gifts. You have gifts bestowed upon you in this lifetime, and when you connect to your soul's purpose and use the gifts in the way you are meant to, money is provided from divine source energy. Abundance is our birthright and we are not meant to struggle. We are meant to experience the luxury and opulence available to us in this human experience. Your money blueprint and abundance codes are already within you.

PAID TO BE YOU WEALTH CODES ACTIVATION

Take a deep breath, close your eyes and allow yourself to be present in this moment connected to divine source energy and repeat:

I activate the money codes already within me. The codes that have been dormant. I feel my DNA being activated as I release any past and present beliefs around money. I feel my gifts are being used in the way that they are meant to. I am creating a ripple effect of change. I activate my money codes. I activate my money codes. Money flows to me with ease. It is safe to receive large amounts of money.

CREATING A PATHWAY FOR MONEY

Money follows on the path of least resistance. If you believe that money flows to you from your corporate job or a partner, that is the way money will flow. There are countless ways to make money. I have more ideas than I have time to implement at this stage!

What if you believed that whatever you sell makes money and that it's easy to make money. Money comes from many sources in your life. Creating aligned programs, making investments, and other ways that you can receive money is a way of life.

I love to receive daily sales in my business. It is something that my business has been set up for. There are programs that are passive income generating programs, payment plans, and semi-passive income. My intention is that money works for me and is received from many sources.

Journal Prompts

- What do you believe about how money will come to you?
- What do you believe is the easiest way for you to make money?
- If you stopped making it hard and allowed receiving money to be a natural part of your life, what would you do differently?
- How do you want money to work for you now?

RELEASING MONEY

As you make more money and are able to receive at a higher level, you also need to be comfortable with releasing money, knowing that even more will come in. There have been so many stages of this in my journey. I remember the first time I invested in a coach, it was a $10K investment. I was petrified—not only was it scary to invest at that level, but it was the first time I had debt. I took out a business loan to fund the investment, after being too afraid to invest prior to this because I didn't want to use my savings. I don't believe that we always have to be paying a business coach or investing in our business—if it feels aligned and it is an energetic match, go through your decision making process as an informed CEO. If it is the decision you want, create or find the resources. Money is always there.

I went on to invest and released $60K in cash in 2018. Within the next month, my savings was back to where it was before. I believe wholeheartedly that when I release money, more comes in to replace it. If we are afraid of letting it go, we are saying to the Universe that we don't trust that it is in infinite supply. What is the point of making millions if you're afraid of investing and spending it? Play with what you would spend the money on if you had $3 million/year in your business. Go wild with the desires you have.

I believe that the more abundantly I live, the more abundance I receive. Money loves purpose and it's meant to be distributed. If I had thought the $10K investment would never come back, I would still be stuck in a soul-sucking corporate job. We need to be willing to trust money and that it always shows up for all of our desires.

Take a moment to reflect on an investment you have made:

▷ What investment have you made that has come back tenfold?

- ▷ How did you show up for that investment?
- ▷ What did you learn about investing in yourself?

PLAY WITH MONEY

Money really gets a bad rap. I'm sure you've heard this a million times: *money is the root of all evil.*

This couldn't be more false.

When I was healing my relationship with money, I put money underneath my bed sheet. Every night when I hopped into bed, I would say, "I am rolling in money!" It made me laugh and really brought me back to how abundant I was.

It's fun to play with money, play with expanding wealth, and treat it less seriously. Make the way you sell fun! Every time a client signs on with you, have fun, play with your manifestations, and play with dreaming even bigger. Allow yourself to play with your profits and honour the desires that you have.

LIVING AS IF

To shift our thoughts, beliefs and energy so that we shift our current reality, it is great to start playing and living as the next level version of you. Start to feel into the edges of expansion and what that looks like for you.

When I first started *living as if,* I would walk down streets with big homes I loved and be in the energy of abundance. I would go into Louis Vuitton, Gucci and Chanel and look at bags—not buying them (yet), but knowing it would happen. *Living as if* quickly became my reality. Being able to walk into a Gucci store and buy whatever I want. Live on an estate filled with millionaires.

When I first started my business, a lot of coaches were advocating travelling business class or having a high-end photoshoot to attract soul clients. It was the norm in the industry and coaches were wracking up tons of debt from a space of "I need to have this to look successful." As they went further from their truth, the fear, scarcity and imposter syndrome kicked in. There were a lot of strange things happening at that time and many of those clients ended up coming to me to detox from the rules, and come back to their truth. That is why I will never advocate a one-size-fits-all approach, cookie cutter programs, or buying things that aren't aligned just to look successful on the outside. You want to feel amazing on the inside, and wealth is a natural byproduct of you being fully expressed and sharing your gifts with the world.

I remember a client asking me if she had to buy a Kate Spade or Louis Vuitton to look successful. I asked her if she wanted to wear those brands offline. Her answer was a resounding *no*. I told her that what clients really resonate with, is you being all of you. No facade, no mask, and no pretending. Vulnerability and authenticity is essential for lasting success.

As the cost of Facebook ads increased and we were required to show up more on Facebook Live and Instagram Stories in an authentic way—no more pretending to be something we were not—the bubble burst. Sadly, many great coaches left the industry because they had gone into too much debt, they were stuck in comparison, or they felt unworthy. "I will never be enough if I can't keep up with Sally down the road."

Newsflash: you are not meant to be like anyone else online. You are an original, and are as unique as your thumb print.

Show up for your soul desires and make them happen, but don't get caught up in the *shoulds, have-to*'s or *must-do's*. Anyone that tells you that you need to be someone else to be successful—run far away. Be more you.

There are moments that *living as if* shifts you. When the cost of Facebook ads went up, I was afraid to increase the budget, although I knew that this was an aligned action. If you can sustain the budget or increase it while others can't, it does put you at an advantage and eventually as the bubble bursts, the cost will also be driven down. Multiple times, I increased the budget for my ad spend and then decreased it out of fear, even though it was aligned to the multi-million dollar version of myself. You don't have to have Facebook advertising, but I've found it incredible to amplify my message and automate my lead generation.

Remember: your soul clients are already in your vortex, ready to pay you whatever you charge! By taking the aligned and guided action in faith, we allow whatever we desire to be manifested in the physical realm. A client I worked with believed that she didn't have to do any marketing on social media, she still had $40K+ months. She is a gifted sales coach and works behind the scenes for big coaching companies. People love the way she does sales calls so much that they connect with her to support them with their sales. There is no one-size-fits-all approach, but you do need to take the aligned action you are guided to take.

▷ **If your business was already generating multi-millions, what are the actions you would take?**

▷ **What have you put off because you are afraid of releasing money?**

Living in a beautiful home with ample space for work and living is important to me. We spend a lot of time at home. When I moved to Bali in 2017, we weren't replacing both of our corporate incomes, but when I looked at homes, there was one that stood out to me. It was beautiful but also the most expensive. We could make payments, but I was not prepared to sacrifice or skimp on other things. Instead, I decided that money simply increases to match my desires. The other places I didn't like, but this was a *hell yeah*! I said yes to the home I really wanted, and the next month, we doubled our revenue and exceeded our corporate salaries. Who knows what would have happened if we took the other place, but I have enough evidence to know that when I say yes to my desires and soul, my soul says yes to me. When something is important and you know it is meant for you, stretching slightly to the next level of desires will shift your income too.

If you keep saying "I would love to, but I can't afford it," you'll receive more of this in your reality. You'll attract more people who can't afford your services and perpetuate the same cycle of lack of money. We can *always* find money for all of our desires and money will increase for what we desire—it is simply energy.

Instead of lowering your standards, expect more to show up and allow money to exceed your desires. I always have more than enough for all of my desires. This goes for everything I buy: clothes, jewellery or items for the house. I no longer go for the cheapest option, I go for what I want. It doesn't mean I always buy designer clothes—I love less expensive items too—but it has to fit nicely and be something I love wearing.

DEBT IS NOT BAD

Growing up, I was taught that you shouldn't live beyond your means, and that debt was bad. It is one of the reasons a lot of us don't invest in ourselves when we know we need it. It was part of the reason why I waited to invest in my first business coach—I was scared of releasing my savings and not having money left.

Had I chosen to invest in myself sooner, I could have saved a lot of time and money. However, I didn't choose to invest in myself until I was back in a corporate job. I took out a $10K business loan and paid it off over time. It was, of course, divinely guided, because I was able to unlearn my limiting beliefs around debt and get support which changed the trajectory of my life. I was so scared of debt before, and in this process, I realised it's not bad at all when we consciously pay for things that support us. It's just a way to pay for things over time.

If you have the debt, drop the guilt around it. Forgive the investments or spending that you did. Instead of focusing on the debt and worrying about how to repay it, focus on all the incredible ways you can make money.

Shifting your beliefs around money is a pivotal part of this process. If you believe that you are bad with money and that everyone has debt, this will be your reality. I prefer to believe that I always have more than enough to save, to invest, to give back freely, to pay my expenses, and honour my soul desires. So it is.

MONEY IS LOVE, LOVE IS MONEY

"Since money is energy, our financial affairs tend to reflect how our life energy is moving. When your creative energy is flowing freely, often your finances are as well. If your energy is blocked, your money does too."

— SHAKTI GAWAIN

- ▷ When you think about money, how do you feel in your body?
- ▷ What are the words that come to mind?

How would it feel different to see money as love, as a tool for freedom, expansion and impact, instead of an enemy or something you need to fear. It is time to allow the fear of money to fall away and come back to love.

When you learn to normalise money, understand that abundance is all around us, and know that it is neutral and like the air you breathe, you make money. Money and miracles want to come into your life. Like you receive each breath you take, allow yourself to receive an overflow of money as a natural process of who you are and the gifts that you have been given in this lifetime. You are meant to enjoy this human experience.

Close your eyes, take a deep breath, and feel your heart expanding. What if you simply made money as beautiful and effortless as the breath you just took? That you, being all of you as you are, was worthy of divine compensation?

If money is love and love is money, then doing more of what you love will make you a vibrational match without the hustle and sacrifice. Think about all the moments in your business when you sell something you're excited about and believe in, and you share it in the way you are guided to. How is it different when you force yourself to create and sell something because you have to?

It is only when we try to overcomplicate and exhaust ourselves or try to push through with things that we *should do*, that receiving money feels hard.

Remember, money is unconditional love. There are no conditions. You can make money if you're sick, unhappy, going through tough personal circumstances, or tired. Money still loves to come into your life. Don't create rules that you have to feel a certain way to receive money—but of course, having it all comes with dialling up every area of your life.

Money is a powerful flow. It is shakti energy. *Shakti* means power, energy, or force. At its most valued and aligned, it is a balance between the masculine (structure, systems and planning) and the feminine (creativity, intuition). It is a Universal Truth that alignment and abundance is the result of the balance between the feminine and the masculine. Create your savvy business structures, hire an accountant, and set up your business bank account. At the same time, embody the creative and embodied flow of receiving money in a sacred and divine way.

The old paradigm of *you have to work hard and hustle for money* is not true. You expand your energetic container to receive more through love, fun and pleasure.

A reminder: money doesn't make you greedy, selfish or a bitch. It is not the root of all evil. When you make a lot of money, you don't turn into someone that you aren't. Money only amplifies what is already within you. If you desire to make a difference in the world and have a larger impact, money allows you to give back freely, not have to worry about your expenses, and to provide even more valuable content to your audience.

Normalise having more than enough for all that you desire without attaching what you make to your self worth. It is amazing what you'll see happen in your life.

I love money and money loves me! This is true for you too.

Soul Reflection

- Where am I judging others around money? What loving thoughts can I now hold and bring into my awareness?
- If money is love how would I now view how I invest, save and spend my money?
- How would it feel to have more than enough money for all that I desire?
- What would change in my life if I allowed money to flow with ease?
- What am I getting from not being rich?
- Why is it not safe to receive more than enough each month?

Remember, everything has a positive payoff. More money for me meant having to manage money. It means getting comfortable with releasing large amounts with buying a home (and actually being tied down after years of travelling and working in different locations around the world). Buying the home comes with a fear of making the wrong decision, as it is a huge investment.

But everything is working for you and you can't make wrong decisions.

We can't ask for 10 more clients or $100K months and in the same breath say "I'm exhausted," "I don't have time," or "I can't support clients."

Get your thoughts and feelings in alignment with what you want.

Get Paid To Be Authentically You

My business journey started with me being unhappy and not aligned in a 9-5 design job. I felt like I had more to give, and the projects I was working on didn't feel right. I felt like this job was draining me creatively. I started my business through a leap of faith and left my 9-5, not knowing where it would go, but knowing I needed to do it. I wanted to have something for myself and do creative work that was exciting to me.

I have felt that I couldn't be paid to be me in the past because I thought that, frankly, I wasn't interesting enough or good enough for someone to want to pay me for what I offer. I felt that I needed to be special somehow, but I didn't feel like I was that. I came from a very average background with a lot of trauma, and I thought that I needed to be 'together' for people to pay me for being me. I spent years doing a lot of work that was not aligned and very forced. I marketed myself in a way that I thought was acceptable and hid behind this for a long time. Despite having my own business, the work I was accepting was not fun at all, and the biggest jobs I had that made me the most money were the jobs I hated the most. I thought that I had to do jobs I hated to make more money. I became complacent with that idea.

The significant shifts that have happened have been around me accepting myself and trusting my path. I have found most of this knowledge and healing through art and in nature. The most significant shift I will discuss was when I went into covid lockdown in Perth, and I didn't know what would happen. I lost all control, lost work, and the only thing I could do was go outside into nature and embrace what was happening. Finally, I realised that no matter what was going to happen with my business, I am held, I am looked after, and I am enough.

This profound shift started the journey to being paid to be me. I then realised that because no matter what I did, I would be OK and that I may as well be ME in my personal life and business. I may as well live in a way that I want to—this means running a business in an authentic way to me, working with clients that are aligned, providing services that are aligned and showing up in a way that is aligned with me and my values—being paid to be me.

By slowly unravelling, allowing and accepting myself as I am, I have started to make different decisions within my business. One of these decisions was to work with Vanessa. Something magical happens when you listen to your gut and invest in yourself and your business. Vanessa has opened up space physically and energetically for me to be supported and thrive simply by being me. I would say to anyone wanting to join Vanessa's program: if you feel like it's right for you, DO IT.

TALEA PATEMORE, Designer & Creator
www.instagram.com/creatrixcreativestudio

chapter 8

Expanding Your Energetic Capacity To Receive

"Everything is energy and that's all there is to it. Match the frequency of the reality you want and you cannot help but get that reality. It can be no other way."
—ALBERT EINSTEIN

I have been obsessed with energy for a long time. I started to notice that when I was excited, happy, relaxed, and doing things I loved in business (as well as honouring myself and my emotions), things came easily to me. When I was in a state of flow and engrossed in the enjoyment of what I was creating, it felt like time expanded. I noticed I was able to create more in a lot less time. This fascinated me, although it was always hit and miss. Things would feel easy and in flow but soon enough I was creating exhaustion, fear and overwhelm.

I was terrified of being "bad" (a deep, limiting belief about myself), and even more terrified of the emotions I associated with that. If I felt "bad" emotions like anger, sadness or frustration, I'd do anything I could to frantically change my emotional state. I was constantly trying to make myself happy through doing: dancing, exercise, walking. Of course, these things are great, but you don't have to force a morning routine to feel happy.

When you look within and choose happiness now, you awaken. Happiness is not a destination. It is not a place you go to when you get X or achieve Y. It is a choice you can make now. When you take aligned actions from happiness and what you love, instead of what you should or must it is incredible what changes.

Instead of "I have to exercise so that I don't put on weight," ask your delicious body: *how do you want to move today? What would bring you joy?*

Instead of "I have to do that Facebook Live today" ask yourself: *what would bring me joy today in my business?* What lights you up, lights up the world.

Take a deep breath in: *I am happy to be alive. I am happy to have this gift of life. I am happy I get to be here.*

On the exhale: *I release the past and let myself live freely in the present while I create a magical future.*

Have you ever felt depleted when you're pushing yourself to do things or started following someone else's strategies for your business success? Have you thought that visibility is about how much content you put out there daily? Do you think that the more you do, the more you will get?

I've been there—giving my power to something external to me. Thinking that the harder I work and the more I do, the more money I make. I thought that I had to show up more. But, it is not about doing more. It is about the energy behind what you're doing. It is the energetic commitment to what you want.

You can say you want 10 clients, but if your energy says, "Don't come near me, I have too much going on," that's what will translate. When you walk into a room, you can feel someone's aura and their presence. The same is true when you are showing up online: people can *feel your presence.* Your energy and aura do your marketing for you—you can't fake it until you make it. You need to heal it to activate it!

In this chapter, I'll share how I shifted my energy, healed my nervous system, and expanded time so that you can too. You *can* feel true inner peace and happiness. This isn't about trying to manic-manifest by obsessing over your goals, pretending to be happy, and doing what you should, have to, or must. This is about cultivating a deep inner knowing that anything your desires are already taken care of, and all that you're ever required to do is be more *you.* How much safer and more powerful does that feel?

If everything is energy, what is more likely to attract what you want?

a. Feeling at peace and confident that you are more than enough. Honouring yourself and your emotions and allowing the flow of life. Not being on 24/7 or forcing yourself to do things.

OR

b. Being needy, creepy, or obsessive about the outcome. Working yourself to a state of burnout, over giving, and always being on.

For whatever reason, the second option may be running the show right now. I want you to allow yourself to see where you may be showing up in that energy and recognise any patterns, any thoughts, and any new awarenesses you now have.

Our culture teaches us that we are not enough as we are. Living in a capitalist society engrains deep beliefs that we are not pretty enough, smart enough, or interesting enough. We have been conditioned to believe that the only way to make money is to work really hard and sacrifice yourself.

It is time to leave these old, boring beliefs behind, awaken your truth, and get paid to be you.

The clients who are out there, willing and excited to pay you, are already in your vortex. They're ready to pay the real you. The you that owns your brilliance, takes care of yourself, and has incredible boundaries. To shift the quality of clients, go deeper into you, rather than further away.

You may have subconscious belief patterns that tell you to work harder and do more. You may have a productivity wound telling you that the more you do, the more worthy and loveable you are. Maybe you have a fear of abandonment telling you others will leave you if you are too much, too loud, or too clever.

The truth? The gig is up. You can't hide any longer. The cracks are appearing. Your true self is being revealed. People-pleasing is falling away and you are rising up and leading as you were born to.

Gently whisper to yourself or shout out loud...

I call back my power. I own my truth. I am a divine being. I am meant to be paid to be all of me.

First, to cultivate a bit more belief here, let's start with some science. I know you like a bit of evidence!

QUANTUM PHYSICS & COLLAPSING TIMELINES

Time isn't linear like we've been led to believe. In the quantum model of the world, there are several different versions of reality simultaneously playing out at any given time, at the same time. That means there is no gap between where you are and the bigger vision you have of yourself.

To "collapse" a timeline, you merely need to understand that all of these versions of reality (and you) are accessible to you at any given time. Linear time isn't actually as big of a factor as we have been led to believe.

What this means is that you can choose how you want your reality to be. You can choose that making money means hard work, but it takes as much energy to believe that money flows to you with ease and the more fun you have, the more money you make. Those realities and versions of you already exist in the quantum realm of infinite possibilities.

Start being like, thinking like, and showing up like the version of you *over there* that already has what you want, and you'll close the "space" between that timeline and your current timeline. The quantum field responds to who we are—not to what we want, or to our thoughts alone. Our thoughts send an electrical signal out into the field. The feelings we generate magnetically draw events back to us.

How we think and how we feel create a state of being. This generates an electromagnetic signature (our aura), which in turn influences everything in our world. If our intentions and desires haven't produced the outcome that we want, then we are sending mixed messages into the field. We're feeling one way and thinking another way. When the body and mind are in opposition we are unable to manifest what we say we want.

Let's create a coherent and consistent message so that you can be a vibrational match for whatever you want, with faith rather than this frantic and downright exhausting stuff.

Here's a list of what has really expanded my energetic capacity to receive love, joy, money, connectedness, and to be able to hold more space for clients and their own transformations. It has also been key to shift from 3D to 5D consciousness.

1. Heal the emotional body through identifying, expressing and releasing anger, rage and grief. To be able to live with integrated feelings and hold the full range of emotions: no more "good" or "bad" polarity.
2. Release drama created through unhealed emotions and inner child wounds.
3. Return to unconditional love for ourselves and others and to open our heart centre.
4. Release judgment of ourselves and others by deeply knowing ourselves.

5. Get to know and have compassion for the shadow self, and integrate the shadow to experience a new level of love and wholeness (More in Chapter 9).
6. Balancing your evolved masculine and feminine energy and connecting back to your natural rhythms and cycles (More in Chapter 10).

Let's go through these in more detail, so that you can shift your consciousness and expand your energetic capacity to receive.

1. FEELING YOUR EMOTIONS IS FREEING

I was a real judgy bitch of my emotions and myself. When I was happy, excited or achieving, I was "good" and when I was sad, emotional or angry, I was "bad." This runs so deep and is extremely common in our society. Instead of pushing away fear, shame, guilt and anger, try honouring and speaking to them.

The next time you have a strong emotion come up, ask yourself:

▷ What am I feeling?

E.g. I feel angry.

▷ Why do I feel angry?

E.g. I feel angry because I wanted to launch a program and I didn't. I feel angry that my period started and I didn't have any energy. I'm angry that I didn't follow through.

- ▷ What is the anger showing me?

    E.g. The anger is showing me that I really do want to launch this program. That it is meant for me.

- ▷ What is the gift in my anger?

    E.g. I realised that I actually wanted this more than I thought. I'm going to use this anger and get that program out there!

- ▷ What are the next steps I am guided to take?

It's not weak to show emotions. It's a brilliant way to release blocked energy in your body and to cultivate emotional intelligence. We need to truly feel the emotions to heal ourselves.

Emotional intelligence (EI) is the ability to understand and manage your own emotions, and those of the people around you. People with a high degree of EI know what they're feeling, what their emotions mean, and how these emotions can affect others.

I feel this emotion because of...

Vs.

Why am I feeling this? It's ridiculous!

This emotion means...

Vs.

I hate this feeling, why do I always do this? I'm so weak.

I was raised in a household where *just getting on with it* was a way to cope with what was happening in the family.

Later when I started my HR career, a boss told me that *crying made me weak.* I didn't cry for six years—but I did do a lot of overspending, binge eating, and drinking. Ultimately, I was doing anything and everything I could to numb the emotions that I wasn't expressing.

Obviously, that didn't work for me (and I'm sure it hasn't worked for you, either). First, it's crucial to unlearn all of the unhealthy beliefs you learned about emotions from your childhood and/or throughout your adult life. By facing these beliefs, you can reparent and heal the child inside of you that still believes it's unsafe to express.

▷ How would you treat yourself or/ your child from a space of unconditional love?

It's time to free yourself from thinking you're messed up or "bad" because you have emotions.

You're a divine, incredible and beautiful being. When you own all of your emotions and receive the gift in all of them, you truly come alive. You can deeply feel sadness and still feel excited. You can be angry and still manifest.

Don't make your emotions or state mean that you can't have something. The more deeply you honour how you feel and give yourself unconditional love in whatever is happening, the more you remain present in the juiciness of life.

ANGER RELEASE RITUAL

When I first started recognising my emotions and fully honouring them, I learned that I had a lot of stored anger and resentment. This showed up in unhealthy ways—lashing out at others, getting really angry with technology, and holding resentment towards family members. Holding deep emotions in our body without processing can have an impact on your health, happiness and cash flow. This ritual has been powerful for me to truly feel the anger and release it.

STEP 1: *Take out a piece of paper and write out everything you are angry about. Allow yourself to rage on that page. No holding back. Write for as long as is needed.*

STEP 2: *Burn the page, with the intention to release the anger.*

STEP 3: *Move as you desire/dance if needed/cry/have a bath or write out what you're grateful for.*

Pleasure, Fun And Joy Are Great For Business

I used to think that I had to work really hard to make money. My life was filled with thinking about and doing work 24/7. Yes, I love my work and what I get to do, but it wasn't from pleasure and fun, it was deeply rooted in fear. I was terrified of being broke and losing it all. I thought that if I peddled harder and faster without leaving my desk, somehow I would feel safe. Somehow those fears would leave me.

I now know the opposite is true. The more I fixate on the outcome and do things that I should, must or have to, the more stress and unhappiness I create. The more I do things from a space of fear, the more fear I create.

That paradigm led me to burnout. If you've been there too, let's not go back there, please.

I had to find a better way.

Did you know that you have 8,000 nerve endings in your clitoris designed for pleasure? *Your pleasure.* We don't need a clitoris to procreate or for any other reason except pleasure. You are a walking divine pleasure vessel. You can't deny that when you have an orgasm, life feels more exciting, things shift, and there is more flow. And if you are created with a clitoris, why would it be there if you were not meant to experience pleasure? It is like having a hand and denying that you need to use it.

Pleasure and more orgasms are great for business! Pleasure, fun, joy and creating what excites you expands your energetic capacity to receive. If you want more clients and cash, have more pleasure!

You don't need to have someone else to provide pleasure. Masturbation and self-pleasure is not a dirty secret you may have been made to believe. It is amazing, it is natural, and it allows you to reconnect to your body and senses. Life is not meant to be filled with struggle and pain (although it is within the realm of possibility if you decide). I truly believe living this human experience is meant to be fun, pleasurable and exciting.

Pleasure extends further than sex and masturbation. (Although, who doesn't love a bit of sex talk!) Being paid to be you definitely needs to come with a warning. You may start to feel super turned on, tuned in, and attract exactly what you want. In fact, let's set the intention that you will.

Time to reflect:

- ▷ How can you create more pleasure in the way you eat?

  Sensual eating, truly slowing down to taste your food, creating a beautiful meal and savouring every mouthful instead of rushing through it or eating what is meant to be "healthy." What do you really love to eat? How can you create more of a sensual and erotic experience with your food?

- ▷ How can you create more pleasure in your work?

  How can you slow down to be present with the gift of doing this work? Instead of doing work to tick a box, do the things that you're guided to do, share the message that you are guided to, and come alive with being you.

- ▷ How can you create more pleasure in the way you dress?

  I love the feelings of different fabrics, beautiful lingerie and bright colours. I love being noticed and standing out—not because I need to, but because it's fun.

- ▷ How can you create more pleasure in the way you have sex?

  Slowing down to allow the pleasure and time to feel the beauty of this energy exchange. "I receive this pleasure."

- ▷ How can you create more pleasure in the way you lovingly move your body?

How often do you exercise because you should or because you want to punish yourself for overeating? Moving your body, moving your energy, and connecting to your body is a loving act. Your body wants to move, it wants to sweat, and it wants to release. How do you love to move your body? Instead of creating rules for the way you should exercise to get an outcome, move because you love it.

Being Turned On & Honouring Your Desires

How deeply do you allow yourself to feel the cravings and turn-ons of life? How deeply do you allow yourself to feel the passion of the work you do, the pleasure of moving your hips when you dance, or the pure magic of sex?

So often we're running on auto-pilot. Doing, doing and more doing without feeling. Not slowing down to actually honour the calling of your desires and deepest turn on.

There are too many female entrepreneurs with a lack of libido, wondering why they can't magnetise clients to them. You don't have to go and find clients, they can feel your energy a mile away when you're in a state of passion, desire and turn-on.

Perhaps you don't even know what turns you on, because conditioning has taught you that sexuality is "bad" or "naughty."

It is time to leave that belief in the dust and explore *you.*

Soul Reflection

- What turns me on? It is time to own your deepest desires: permission to get saucy.
- What feels exhilarating in my business?
- What edgy, naughty and erotic thing do I secretly want to share? Then go share it!
- How good will it really feel to unleash all of me in the world?

2. BREAKING UP WITH DRAMA

Drama distracts us from our truth and is deeply rooted in survival mode patterns, often happening completely unconsciously. It is also linked to self-sabotage and staying in the familiar. I loved creating drama in my life. Drama around client calls, around doing live training, around writing a post, around clients saying no, and everything in my life. It created a lot of exhaustion which was what I was familiar with.

The pattern went like this: I would fill my schedule with client calls, feel exhausted, and have a tantrum. "This is hard, why do I have to do this," and with that, I would disconnect from my higher self and want to pack up my bags and live in an Ashram in India. Whenever life felt great or things were coming to me with ease, it felt unfamiliar. Unconscious to these patterns, I would pick a fight or perpetuate this cycle. Exhaustion kept me safe and small. It kept me in the familiar.

How did I break the cycle of exhaustion and drama?

- I owned where I was creating drama in my life. Often, when we have a deep fear of not being good enough, we don't want to see our flaws. Until we bring this to the surface and really see it, we can't heal it. Awareness is key.
- I realised that I had set my business and life up for exhaustion. I had created a schedule where I had calls one after the other with no space for rest.

▷ Where have you created a business set up for exhaustion?

▷ If you were setting yourself up for vibrancy, what would you now do?

▷ What would your day look like?

- When I felt like I wanted to tantrum, I loved, honoured and held my afraid inner child. I asked myself: "Vanessa, what do you need right now to fully honour yourself?" Food, sleep, rest, sex are basic needs. When you feel like you're overwhelmed it is not the space to push harder, it is the time to slow down.
- Creating the shift from *I have to,* to *I get to*. I decided to really celebrate every client call, sales call, and training I got to do. Once I had listened to my inner child, I had to make decisions from my adult self. If there were activities that needed to be done, sometimes I would need to connect to how it would feel to have them completed and create the discipline of creating what I needed.

3. OPENING YOUR HEART & RETURNING TO LOVE

How you received love growing up is likely how you show love to others and to yourself. For most of us, love was given conditionally. We have learned that love is earned by being a certain way.

Being one of four children in a household with mental health challenges brought a dynamic that wasn't optimal for receiving unconditional love. My siblings and I all tried to get love and attention in different ways. For me, I thought that achieving, getting great grades and excelling at sports equated to love. Unfortunately, most of what I did was never good enough so I kept pushing, proving, and trying harder.

You Are Not What You Achieve

These patterns followed me into my career and business. I created a belief that I am only worthy if I achieve, make money, and am Facebook Live ready 24/7.

How you received love as a child is an important lens to look through. It is likely where you are only showing yourself love now. Do you only feel happy and loveable and worthy when you get a new client, make a sale, or have something material to show?

When you bring this into your business, happiness and self-worth still becomes dependent on achieving and getting the next client.

With your clients, you need to be cautious of mothering them in the way you were brought up. Some clients will look to you as a mother figure and often, if we are not conscious of it, we can assume the same role as our own mother or the opposite. If you judge clients for only achieving a certain "good girl" result, but aren't able to hold the space and celebrate every shift, we are running our business from ego instead of love.

Soul Reflection

- Where am I treating myself like I was treated growing up?
- How am I showing up for my clients in this way?
- If I were to reparent and love myself unconditionally, what would that look like?
- If I came from a place of unconditional love with clients what would that now look like?

The key to this is remembering that you are loved as you are. You are worthy as you are. You are a success as you breathe, and achieving something external to you makes you no less or no more worthy.

The doing is simply an extension of your most fully expressed self. When we start to separate our self-worth from our business, we can finally detach from outcomes. We can have a launch that doesn't go fully to plan and still enjoy our life. We can have someone say no on a sales call and still enjoy our life.

Love As The Portal To Expansion

The more love you can show yourself through reparenting, honouring your emotions, and following through on what you desire to create, the more love expands. Love heals, and when we have the space to hold our clients in a sacred space of love, it is incredible what shifts can take place.

▷ **What can change in your life with a heaping dose of love and belief?**

I remember a point in my business where I linked my worthiness to what my clients were making in *their businesses.* All of my worthiness was wrapped up in how many sales I made, how much I achieved in a day, and the "good" things my clients did.

Obviously, this was exhausting, and my emotions were like a rollercoaster, dependent on external factors. What's worse is I was judging their experiences through the lens of my unhealed and ego self. Your soul clients need to have their journey, and we can't fix or save them (they're not broken). What they really need is zero judgement, allowing their individual process, and reminding them of their brilliance.

In my business, I get *so many* positive testimonials. I have 2000+ messages of praise and past clients keep reaching out to say how the work we've done has shifted them!

Here are some things to remember when working with clients:

- Don't make it about your ego and your craving for worthiness from a deep-seated need to be loved. We think that we "care" and we are doing it for our clients, but often it is for ourselves.
- Your clients create their results themselves, and you are the guide and mirror for their evolution. Hold space for all of the juiciness without judgement while simultaneously believing in their bigger vision. They do the work and show up. These aren't your results to feed your ego with.
- You are worthy and loved FULL STOP. They are worthy and loved FULL STOP. *If you made all decisions from a space of worthiness, faith and love, what would change?*

- Believe in your clients no matter what. They can create anything. Belief is the foundation for shifting your reality.
- The more you love yourself and have an overflow of love for clients, the more love you receive.

Love is incredibly powerful.

▷ Where can you show yourself more love today?

▷ What would love create?

Honouring Your Basic Needs

Part of healing and nourishing your inner child is to fully honour yourself. If your basic needs were not met growing up, you may find imbalances in the way you care for yourself.

When I was recovering from burnout, the Reiki healer I was working with kept saying to me when I felt exhausted that I needed to get back to basics. The basics are: water, sleep, exercise, eating and going to the loo.

▷ How often do you overwork and not honour those basic needs? How often do you push through when you are tired? How often do you not eat when you feel hungry?

This is a foundational piece of coming back to balance and honouring yourself.

Creating Loving Boundaries

I was unaware of how terrible I was with boundaries until a therapist informed me. It was actually shocking how little boundaries I had—physical, energetic, emotional and mental. I was the dumping ground for everyone's stuff and deep down it made me feel loved, worthy and useful. Hearing the ping of a Voxer or message from a client made me feel like I was of value. I was still needing external validation to fill the deep wound of not feeling good enough.

If you're always on, always answering messages, and not allowing your clients to think for themselves, you aren't empowering them—you're enabling them. Everyone has the answers within them. It was a hard realisation to face. Having a lack of boundaries wasn't actually serving me or my clients. In fact, it was setting a poor example of what honouring yourself really looks like.

Boundaries and setting clear agreements and terms is the most loving thing you can do for your clients and your team.

Soul Reflection

- What loving boundaries do I need to put in place if I own that I am more than enough?
- What would be different if I empowered my clients to think for themselves instead of thinking I know better than them?

Where am I allowing myself to be physically, mentally and emotionally drained? Where do I need to say NO?

4. RELEASING JUDGEMENT

I used to judge everything and everyone! I thought that women were too loud, too pretty, too thin, too fat and too confident. All the things I felt uncomfortable with inside of me. With this came difficulty with interacting with friends and other women. I saw them as competition.

When we feel out of control, we want to blame other people for our discomfort. Judgement is one of our most addictive patterns, and we love to perpetuate these addictive patterns unless we consciously shift them.

For years, I tried to rationalize or dismiss what seemed like innocent enough behavior. We get a quick hit of self-righteousness when we judge others. When we feel hurt, insecure or vulnerable, it is easy to turn to judgement. Our judgments towards others seem to make us feel better than them and give us a hit of feeling smarter, savvier and better.

But, judgement started to disconnect me from the very work I do in the world to empower and lift others up. So I had to heal the parts of me that I was judging others for.

RELEASING JUDGEMENT RITUAL

- Bring your awareness and attention to the judgment you are making. Don't judge yourself for having the thought, but allow yourself to understand where you are judging.
- Connect into how you feel having this judgement and what part of you needs to heal. If you keep judging confident women, what part of you is craving to be seen and heard? If you keep saying someone is stupid, what part of you is afraid to see this within yourself? How are you protecting your wounds?
- Understand where you can connect to love. Extend that love to yourself and anyone you are judging.

- Forgive or pray for the strength to forgive. If you're not there yet, allow yourself to set the intention to allow love and forgiveness in.

  This ancient Hawaiian prayer, **ho'oponopono prayer,** is beautiful for forgiveness:

  "I'm sorry, Please forgive me, Thank you, I love you." That's it. "I'm sorry, Please forgive me, Thank you, I love you."

  It's very touching, especially given how simple and Universal these words are.

  When we heal judgement, we allow love to flow more freely. When we are tapped into love consciousness, we receive more love.

chapter 9

Integrating All Parts Of You, Owning Your Shadow Self & Wholeness

"I'd rather be whole than good."

"The shadow is ninety percent pure gold."

—CARL JUNG

The other day when I was on the toilet taking a poo, I thought to myself: *this is exactly how to demonstrate the shadow!*

You may be thinking: *wow, too much information,* or, *thanks for that image, Vanessa!* Or maybe you're thinking: *good for her. I love a good poo!*

Hear me out. Why is 1 out of 7 people constipated, why will 1 in 4 people experience a mental health problem of some kind each year and why—with so much information and personal development books—are more people obese, unhappy and feeling unworthy?

I truly believe that much of this is linked to the suppression of the Shadow Self.

So back to the poo analogy: it's an amazing feeling having a great bowel movement, but we are told not to talk about and not to share those details. As children we love a good poo story, yet parents tell us that we shouldn't talk about it. We learn that poo is *embarrassing*.

Disease starts in the gut. So why aren't we having more conversations around poo? Why aren't we sharing more about how we feel? Why aren't we more open to holding space for people that are sad, angry and negative, helping develop tools to manage emotions in a healthy way? Why aren't we having more conversations around sex (and having more sex)?

As we learn to be more polite, less outspoken, and told to speak about acceptable things, we start to lose our true essence. It is why most people keep seeking something outside of themselves to feel whole. It is why you may feel broken and in need of fixing, because you aren't seeing the gift in who you are in your *entirety*. You're trying to be good and acceptable while shoving down the wild, weird and different parts, making you feel like an inauthentic phony.

This is how the shadow forms and starts to run our lives. It is our job to recognise, honour, and embrace it.

You are not broken—you simply need to remember your magnificence. The key is seeing all parts of you.

WHY LOVE AND LIGHT WON'T SET YOU FREE

We are bombarded with *love and light* mantras and spiritual bypassing. Shoving down our feelings and slapping an affirmation together that doesn't actually feel true to us creates dissonance and represses parts of us. Although affirmations and other spiritual practices have benefits, it is important to also embrace the shadow.

After battling mental health issues myself and witnessing it in my family—as well as my years of work with clients—I have seen the many ways that the repressed shadow shows up in families, relationships, and daily life. Road rage, binge eating, alcoholism, affairs, overspending, sexual assault, killing people for money, and wars are all ways that the shadow plays out in society. When I started doing shadow work I was able to set myself free, bring back gifts that I had disenfranchised from, and speak my truth. I realised where I was judging what was inside me, and stopped. Allowing full acceptance of all parts of me.

When we develop an idealized self we are unable to see our shadow. We will judge others for their "bad" behaviour, put ourselves on a pedestal for our good deeds, or even fail to see criminals as human.

Because I believed that anxiety was weak, I didn't even notice I had severe anxiety and trichotillomania. Instead, I projected and viewed others with anxiety as weak (while I was internally spiralling and pulling out my hair, totally unaware). Frightening how the shadow plays out.

By looking only at the positive and light side, we are unable to see the beauty and gifts in the shadow. Instead of toxic positivity or spiritual bypassing, it's time to take a deep, hard look at the shadow. It's not easy, but it's exciting: there is so much magic to be discovered!

MEETING YOUR SHADOW SELF

The shadow is the side of your personality that contains all the parts of yourself that you don't want to admit to having. It is the part that you feel ashamed about and often try to hide. The problem with hiding it, unfortunately, is that it amplifies and will soon bite you in the butt!

Much like a beach ball that you keep pushing down under the water so that no one can see, the further it is pushed down, the harder it will smack you in the face. Let's not continue to push it down. Let's free the beach ball! I promise: it's safe to be all of you.

For most of us, our shadow is unconscious. It is only through effort to become self-aware that we are able to recognise and integrate our shadow. Although many speak about the shadow as "negative," this could not be further from the truth. The shadow is what you *perceive* as dark and weak about yourself, and therefore needing to be hidden and denied. This varies for everyone, as we all have different perceptions of what is "bad." So while for one person their shadow might contain sadness, rage, laziness and cruelty, you might also hide your personal power, your independence, or your emotional sensitivity in your shadow. It all depends how you've been conditioned.

THE GIFTS IN YOUR SHADOW

I really feared being lazy, and for me, that was the ultimate insult. It was something that was frowned upon in our family. *Rest when you're dead* was something I heard a lot, along with *poor people that do nothing are a drain on society*. This, coupled with my dad leaving home at 4 a.m. to milk the cows and return after dark to put food on the table and clothe our family of six, taught me that work and making money came with exhaustion, sacrifice and long hours.

A result of fearing laziness is becoming overly busy. You'll overwork yourself and be exhausted. You may hold a deep belief that you're only worthy when you're exhausted. We need to create balance in our lives, and being able to actively understand when we need to rest and take time out is important to creating meaningful, authentic work.

On the positive side, I developed a great work ethic. When I need to create something, it gets done. The flip side was burnout and exhaustion. As you can see, the shadow side isn't all bad or dark—in balance, it's powerful. When we embrace the slow, we can fully embrace the speeding up.

You can't *not* have a shadow. No matter how nice or happy someone may seem, they have a shadow side, just like anyone else. In fact, we can't see the light within ourselves and others without being present to the darkness. How can we know what happiness is if we have never felt sadness? Nor can you get rid of or heal your shadow. It's an essential and useful part of you.

Your shadow is something that can indeed offer many gifts of insight and personal power. It is the part of you that when seen and acknowledged, you can create content that illuminates those parts within your clients. You can embrace this part of you and use it as a superpower. It truly is the part of you that will support you with standing out. When you use this in content your soul clients will feel heard, seen and understood on a much deeper level.

It is a win-win, and so incredibly freeing. But it does take looking within and owning all parts of you. It takes questioning what you were taught, so you can evolve into the person you're meant to be.

OWNING MY SHADOW

The realisations about myself doing shadow work are vast.

I'll share the two that have been most profound for me, as they ran my life for a long time.

- Make the money and I'll feel good enough.
- Get skinny and I'll feel good enough.

This is what I had on repeat. However, the more money I made and the more weight I lost, the greater my imposter syndrome grew. The greater the fear of losing it all and being *found out* became.

When I started to actually look at why I felt like I wasn't good enough, everything changed. I learned at a young age that no matter how much I achieved, it wasn't good enough. This was instilled by my well-meaning father, who had similar expectations placed on him growing up. It wasn't uncommon to hear something like: "You did well in that exam but why aren't you top of the class?"

I kept pushing and trying to achieve more. The fear of not being good enough caused me extreme stress about getting good grades, which led to me pulling out my hair when studying. I realised that because I thought I wasn't good enough, I also judged others for not being good enough. I'd bring others down and judge them to boost my ego. On the flip side, I was holding others on a pedestal. If I idolised someone, I'd try to be like *them*. It was exhausting having this inner turmoil.

No one is like you and that is your superpower.

I realised that my father's version of success was different to mine. I had to own that not feeling good enough was not because I wasn't good enough, it was simply because I was trying to follow someone else's (or society's) version of success.

From the age of 13, I went to great lengths to start to fit in, look pretty, and be skinny. I was on diets and started going to the gym at a young age. To feel happy and worthy, I needed compliments from others about my appearance, so I would always dress up. I would weigh myself multiple times a day. I was absolutely obsessed.

My dad sometimes called women "fat bitches" and my mom was on a diet most of her adult life, as she struggled with her weight as a teenager. She often said: "None of my children will be fat." Clearly, being fat was something that was deeply frowned upon in my family, and it created an obsession to be thin so that I could be loved. As my shadow self was repressed even more, I pushed myself further to look a certain way, and when I couldn't push anymore or I got injured, I gave up.

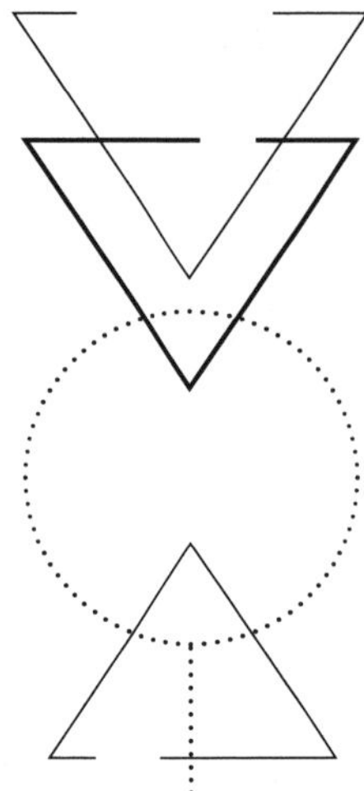

No one is like you and that is your superpower.

Finding balance and loving my body has been a long journey. It is important to look after my health and be active, but I am happy in my body. I move daily and create food that is pleasurable. Actually focusing less on the scale has allowed me to be fitter, leaner and healthier. There is nothing wrong with desiring an incredible physique, but it's important to acknowledge *why* you're obsessed. If you never reach that goal, is your self-worth dependent on it?

If your happiness is based on something external to you and can be taken away, then you need to come back to yourself. What is the point of waiting for something external to be happy?

THE REALISATIONS

Facing my shadow self has provided me with infinite realisations about myself. I realised the things I wasn't good at and had no desire to learn, despite it working for others. I realised and embraced the things I am obsessed with (all the things I talk about in this book), and through embracing those things, learned what I need to focus on in my business. I realised that because of not feeling good enough, I was afraid of looking stupid in training sessions, although I had a deep desire to further my studies. Through facing my shadow, I embraced that I am always the student, always growing and learning, and that I can say silly things and mess up and still be incredible at what I do.

My shadow also showed up as a know-it-all, in an attempt to protect my wound of not feeling good enough. If someone's opinion differed from mine, I'd think they were wrong, and cling on to having to be right. If I was wrong, I would over analyse conversations and shame myself. It is absolutely okay to not know everything—in fact, if you knew everything you wouldn't be on this planet. What would be the point? Keep learning and growing while simultaneously knowing you know enough, are enough, and have enough as you are.

Imposter syndrome is a high achiever's problem—we lack the ability to celebrate and see how far we have come, always thinking we need to do more, be more, and create more—often forgetting how much we have done. As I have spent most of my life trying to overachieve, it has meant that everything I create is at a high standard. The high standard is great, but I don't need to have the not-good-enough energy behind it.

I have found that the key to unlocking and embracing my wholeness is to own all parts of me. To take a magnifying glass on the parts that I am ashamed of, hiding from and frustrated about. To integrate the shadow. To integrate the good girl *and* the nasty, lazy bitch.

I was trying to be what I *thought* perfect was. I was trying to show the outside world a part of me and hide the parts that were not acceptable. I tried to show my parents that I was a good girl by achieving and getting great grades. I was people-pleasing to be liked. Quite frankly, it was exhausting living a double life and a facade.

Remember, you are already perfect. You were born that way. But we spend so much of our lives trying to be like others, trying to have what others have, and trying to look like a model in a magazine. We think that business success comes from being like those that are making a certain amount, when in fact, the most magnetic thing is you being fully you. The magnetism is in your wholeness. In your sovereignty. In owning every delicious part of who you are.

You are perfect as you are with all the so-called "imperfections" that you think you have. In fact, most of our dreaded imperfections are the very things the world needs to see more of. Our superpowers and gifts are trapped in the darkness, shoved away so no one can find them. And the more we try to play different roles to please different people, the more we lose our true essence.

We are living in a conditioned world, pretending to be the polite and acceptable version of ourselves. This creates a separation between who we are and the version of ourselves the outside world sees. There is the mask or persona when we show up on Facebook Live, when we head to a corporate job, or have an interview with someone. The mask we put on with family and some friends. Then there is the behind the scenes: the version of you crying, binge-eating, overspending, masturbating and desiring more pleasure, but not fully owning your desires. Laden with shame, guilt and the parts that you have disowned and shoved down.

The more you wear the masks, the more you dull down and dim down, causing your true essence to feel unworthy, ashamed and unloved. Your true life force energy and spark disenfranchised.

The pathway to true self acceptance, wholeness, magnetism and ultimately being paid to be you is through calling back the lost parts and owning all of your magic.

Shadow work has been deep, disruptive, and profoundly powerful. Truly seeing myself for who I am and owning that anything

I see in someone else that triggers me is within *me*. I didn't say being paid to be you was sunshine and rainbows—it is about remembering who you really are. Releasing the guilt, removing the shame, and recognising that everything that has happened has ultimately been for your growth and evolution.

The "failures" have their gifts.

Laziness has its gifts.

The bitchy seductress has her gifts.

Anger has its gifts.

Debt has its gifts.

Let's start to remove the notion that things are "good" or "bad" or "right" or "wrong." Let's take this journey together to uncover your wild, bold, unapologetic and confident self. Let's peel back the mask and unpeel the layers of the onion.

Let's uncover and unleash the true you—the you who's waiting to be seen, to be heard and to be noticed for your magnificence—so that you can create the ripple effect of change in the world.

Journal Prompts

- Pick an adjective from the list below that would trigger you if someone would use it to describe you, and then ask yourself: "Why would this trigger me? What would be bad about it being true? Is it the accuracy or inaccuracy that bothers me? What could be a positive aspect to being that way?"

LIST: *arrogant, liar, jealous, mean, cruel, possessive, bitchy, bossy, loser, greedy, mysterious, sneaky, sick, fat, disgusting, stalker, stupid, idiot, fearful, unconscious, masochistic, narcissist, insignificant, frigid, sexist, manipulative, racist, victim, arrogant, ugly, careless, passive, aggressive, lame, boring, tactless, irresponsible, incompetent, lazy, unfair, childish, know-it-all, insensitive, psychotic, sad, ordinary, hypocritical, reproachful, gloomy, jealous, envious, dirty, tyrannical, inflexible, heartless, resentful, dominant, bad, ignorant, uneducated, tasteless, insecure, depressed, hopeless, not good enough, cry baby, paranoid, pushy, stubborn, inferior, weak, impatient, unreliable, self-destructive, over-sensitive*

- ▷ Why do you feel an aversion to those words, and why are you ashamed of those situations? Think about where it comes from, who do you think of, or perhaps when you were called this.
- ▷ What could be the GIFT in them?
- ▷ Rename them. If you were to meet in the middle, what is the word you would use? For example, if good girl or whore/slut/ bad girl comes up as a trigger, the middle may be fiercely feminine or assertive.
- ▷ What emotion do you try to avoid (e.g. sadness, jealousy, anger). What makes you afraid to feel this? What will happen if you feel it? What is the gift in that emotion?
- ▷ What do you think is your worst trait? Why is it "bad"? What positive aspects does this trait bring with it?
- ▷ What are you ashamed of? What is your truth?

MIRRORS, PROJECTIONS AND TRIGGERS

Everyone is a mirror for your growth and expansion. We can only see in others what is already within us. That is how the brain works. It means that the things that trigger you and things you admire are both within you.

If you see someone as judgemental or controlling, bring the power back and ask yourself what part of you craves control, or what part of you is being judgemental or controlling?

Get curious. The triggers will awaken you but if you keep blaming others and projecting, you'll miss the growth.

A few years ago, I turned to Shaun and said: "I feel like my Mom is being such a victim, she's not really listening to me." I took a step back and asked myself, *where am I being the victim and not listening to her?* It uncovered a new layer of connection and a softening to the relationship. It helped show me where I was being the victim and blaming instead of taking responsibility for my life. No one else can make us feel less than without our permission.

You can't change others, but you can change yourself.

A nasty comment from someone online only affects us if we believe there is some truth in it. Instead of fearing a troll on the internet, allow yourself to grow from the experience.

I remember someone commented on my Facebook ad saying: "Here's the fraud we have been talking about." At first it felt heartbreaking. There was a part of me that thought I was a fraud. But this was an opportunity to remind myself of my brilliance.

Are you a fraud?

I'm not a fraud, but I do think I may be overpromising on X or not owning my intuitive side.

What is your truth?

My truth is that I do amazing work in the world and I have supported and been a guide for so many soul clients. I need to own my intuitive gifts and use them more in my work. This is what clients are really paying me for.

Whatever we don't own within ourselves tends to be projected on to others. If we don't think we are good enough, we try to find why others are not good enough. If we are being greedy and obsessed around money, we will project it onto others. Be aware of what you are saying about others and look within yourself—this has been one of the hardest and most rewarding ways to heal.

Often clients will say to me: "My partner just doesn't understand me, doesn't show me enough love, and doesn't support me." My question is: "Where are you not supporting them, making them a priority or accepting their differences?" It is always an area that they are not honouring, either. When you see it and own it, you can change it.

Journal Prompts

- What do you admire about someone else? This is within you—allow yourself to see that.
- What triggers you with your mom/dad/sister/friends/clients/partner/husband?

- ▷ What is triggering you online?
- ▷ Where is this within you? What part of you are you denying?
- ▷ What part of you do you need to heal?

INTEGRATING AND EMBODYING THE SHADOW

Remember, the shadow isn't just the wounded part of us—it's also the path towards a more authentic and fulfilling life. It is important to make a distinction between "this is a *part* of me" versus "this is me." In order to heal, repair and grow on a physical, mental, emotional and spiritual level, we need to practice shadow work and be aware of the shadow on a daily basis.

When we start to do shadow work, at first we may feel like we don't know ourselves or that our lives have been a lie. I felt this way at first, but when we peel back these layers, we are then able to connect to our truth.

When you chuck it all up in the air, you can let it land in the way you want to without guilt, judgement or fear.

When I understood where my obsession with money, achievement and my appearance came from, I was able to integrate all of these parts and connect to my truth.

I realised that money is an incredible tool and has provided so much freedom. I know that being rich allows me to give back freely and I believe that I am meant to be rich in this lifetime to be able to do just that.

My truth: money is neither good nor bad; it is like the air I breathe. Having more or less doesn't make me any more worthy or loveable—it simply amplifies what is already within me. I believe that I have desires for a reason and I'm willing to take the actions I'm guided to which automatically creates exactly what I desire. Money flows as an effortless byproduct of me being my authentic self.

But my worthiness and lovability is not linked to how much I make, how much my clients make or how much I do.

I was able to let go of the need to look a certain way and to receive compliments for my appearance to feed my lack of confidence. I now know that if I do put on weight or not look done up on a day, I am still loved.

Journal Prompts

Look at the parts of your life that you have been ashamed of:

- What is your truth? What are you scared to admit?
- What parts are you now ready to embrace?
- What parts of you are you ready to release?
- What are your new beliefs?
- What parts of you are you ready to call back and own?

  E.g. You may lose your desire for sex because of being teased at school for being a slut, you may lose your femininity because you thought you needed to be a man to get ahead, you may desire to speak on stage but you had a traumatic experience. Your greatest gifts are in the shadow and disenfranchised parts of you. Call it all back.

Close your eyes and drop into your body, deep belly breaths as you connect to your core. You can open your eyes with each sentence while you breathe it in.

I call back my disenfranchised self and soul fragments.

I am whole, complete and incredible as I am.

I honour and hold space for every delicious part of me.

I am loved.

I am more than enough.

Having it all is my birthright.

Embracing & Integrating The Shadow Self

I'm Cortney, owner of Life Lived Fearless. I've always had a huge passion for helping other women live fearlessly in pursuit of living their dreams and finding their freedom. Today, my business serves many women who want to align and uplevel both their life and business, through aligned strategy, mindset and energy. However, I quickly found while building my business that I kept hitting roadblocks and playing small. It was frustrating because in other areas of my life (fitness, health and personal goals) nothing held me back. When I put my mind and heart to something, I always made it happen. I live with a rare disease that has a long list of limits, but I don't play victim to it and choose to live without limits. However...I kept placing limits on myself in my business. I was frustrated, overwhelmed and questioning everything.

Then I got connected with Vanessa. I thought I needed the right strategy and all the answers. She quickly showed me all the answers were already within me, I just had to dust off the external world, shut out my ego and return to myself. She taught me how you do one thing in life is how you do everything, in which I began to channel my limitless personality into my business to help others. It wasn't that I needed more, I actually needed less, to shed old patterns and faulty thoughts that were never mine to own.

Deep down the hard truth was I didn't feel worthy enough to be paid to be me. My past relationships and experiences caused me to shove feelings down and ultimately turn my power off.

Vanessa held space and allowed me to dig deep to turn my power back on and up to a level I never thought was possible. I now give myself full permission to ask for more, to live bigger, to love more and to be the ultimate CEO in both my life and biz. I'm able to live the "hell yes" lifestyle I truly desired.

Vanessa's programs are way beyond words, it's more than surface-level and changes every aspect of life. Do it, you need it way more than you know. No more playing small, you have a purpose on earth and you can actually get paid to do it...all while having fun and being you!

CORTNEY JOHNSON

You can find her at www.instagram.com/lifelivedfearless

chapter 10

Balancing The Divine Masculine & Feminine

"There are four main female archetypes that we cycle through during our lives: Maiden, Mother, Wild Woman & Wise Woman. Each archetype corresponds to a different season, a different phase of the moon, and a different phase of our menstrual cycle. These are all connected."

— SHANI JAY

In a world where many women have fallen into the category of "good girl" or "whore," I have found that honouring and integrating the female archetypes that live within me to be profoundly healing.

In my journey towards full self-acceptance and self love, connecting to all the archetypes within me—in addition to working within the phases of my menstrual cycle and the moon's cycles — has helped me accept all the parts of me. As we'll explore in this chapter, each archetype has a light and a shadow side. And don't worry—you don't need to take a goddess bath to connect with the femininity inside of you. (But if you want to, I highly recommend it!)

In my experience as well as culturally and historically, the one archetype that is often neglected is the Wild Woman. The Wild Woman does not align with our patriarchal societies' expectations of how a woman should be, which is why many of us don't allow her to emerge in our lives. The Wild Woman is unapologetic, sensual, uninhibited and often direct. I see a lot of clients in this phase of their cycle (pre-menstrual) disconnect from their wildish ways.

It is time to embrace all parts of you, unapologetically. Let's journey through and connect back to our wild ways, to the natural rhythms of life, and fully embrace being a female.

INTEGRATING AND HONOURING OUR ENERGY

We all have masculine and feminine energy within us, which is not related to gender. Manifestation comes from the balance between the divine masculine and divine feminine energy. Learning to create this balance and flow in business will help with expanding your capacity to receive and create more of an impact. We need both in balance and to operate from the evolved energies, this is key to wholeness.

The right side of your body is masculine (connected to the left side of your brain for logical reasoning) and the left side is feminine (connected to the right side of the brain for creativity).

Intuition, feelings and creativity are characterised by the feminine side of our natures. The masculine side is characterised by logic, facts and systems. If you're giving too much to others to the detriment of yourself, your feminine side may be overactive and your right side may need strengthening. This will be in the form of creating firm boundaries and speaking your truth. If your life is overly rigid and structured, your masculine aspect may be overactive. It will be important to develop your feminine aspect to bring a more creative and flexible approach.

The masculine side gives, and the feminine side receives.

FEMININE ENERGY: Receptive, Passive, Inward, Intuitive, Creative, Receiving, Contractive

MASCULINE ENERGY: Active, Projective, Giving, Expansive, Outward

DIVINE FEMININE	WOUNDED FEMININE	DIVINE MASCULINE	WOUNDED MASCULINE
Unconditional love	Neediness	Confidence	Aggressive
Understanding	Co-dependent	Inner strength	Controlling
Flow	Over-emotional	Focus	Abuse of power
Stillness	Over-sensitive	Logical	Obsession with material things to feed the ego
Able to feel emotions and balance emotions	Addicted to drama	Boundaries	Unstable
Able to receive from the masculine	Manipulative	Support	Unsupportive
Ease	Victim	Clarity	Inability to express emotions
Surrender	Powerlessness	Stability	Unable to give and support the feminine
Radiance	Withholding	Direction	Competitive
Feeling	Overbearing	Capable	
	Flaky	Discipline	
		Assertive	

When I started my business, I was very much in my wounded masculine energy. I was doing, hustling and following all the systems and structures that I "should" to be successful. I was addicted to achievement and obsessed with outcome and material things at the expense of my health and happiness. My divine feminine creativity, play, feeling and flow wasn't honoured or even seen.

Just before burning out, my intuition started to sharpen. I had powerful visions and my connection to self and spirit strengthened. It was amazing.

A client who was eight weeks pregnant hadn't mentioned anything about it to anyone else. One night I woke up with a jolt as I saw a baby in her stomach, with a blue colour surrounding the baby. At this stage she didn't know the sex of the baby. When I asked her, she was in fact pregnant and later had a beautiful boy. Your intuition and ability to connect at this level with those around you is powerful and it is within all of us.

I know burning out was the gift I needed to reconnect to my true self. To honour my intuition and to let my intuition guide me in my business. I've created a divinely feminine-led business, where the masculine structures are intuitively guided, instead of doing things because others are or because I should.

You can't betray yourself and your soul any longer. You can't ignore your intuitive guidance (which we all have), the unexplainable gut feeling, the voice telling you to go deeper on something with a client, or the internal guidance telling you to share a message. It is always there and it gets even louder when we start to listen to the wisdom rather than trying to logic our way through everything. It is why anxiety and being stuck in your head is so prevalent— you're not listening to all the wisdom and taking action on what is important.

When you receive guidance and you leave it alone or disguise it as fluke, you receive less of it and often operate from what you think you should do.

Who am I to lead a movement?

Who am I to help others awaken to their truth?

Who am I to be a messenger?

Sound familiar? The truth is, the more you deny it, the harder it gets. The more challenges you have to redirect you. The more launching you do and non-soul clients you attract that trigger you.

I promise: it is much easier to follow the call of your soul. To follow through on what you're being guided to do. If you hear it and it resonates deeply, it is your truth and it needs to be in this physical plane.

You may feel that you need what someone else has to be "successful" or to have what they have. And the more you deny your gifts and follow someone else's blueprint for success, the more you disconnect from your intuition, your gifts, and your ability to receive divine compensation.

Radical devotion to the things that you are passionate about and are guided to create results in more ease, more flow and more purpose.

The question isn't whether your intuition is strong enough, it is whether you are willing to listen, honour and follow it. To live in alignment with your soul and be all that you're meant to be.

5 WAYS TO CONNECT BACK TO YOUR DIVINE FEMININE ENERGY

1. Take time to listen to your intuition

I love dancing to activate my intuition (although you don't have to *do* anything to activate it). Let the hips gyrate, pull energy through your pussy, and let your soul guide you. I find my best intuitive guidance through naked dancing with my soul. Put your favourite music on and feel the divine feminine juiciness. Slowing down and taking time to tune into your inner wisdom is important.

2. Make space for play, pleasure and creativity

We receive from the feminine and give from the masculine. If you're always giving, taking responsibility for others and striving without giving back, you become burnt out, exhausted and bitter. Because I've been in the space of ambition and high-achieving for most of my life, doing and taking action is natural for me, but slowing down and switching off has been a challenge. It takes discipline. Schedule days where you have nothing to do. Just *be*. Make space for art and creating.

3. Receive

Allow yourself to receive the compliment, the beauty of nature, the breath, the money, the support, and lean back and allow yourself to receive sexual pleasure.

4. Sensuality

Any activity can become sensual if you intentionally experience it with all five senses. Feel the water in the bath and make it a beautiful pleasure practice. When you make food, create a beautiful sensual experience.

5. Feel Your Emotions

Feeling and managing your emotions is key to activating the divine feminine. Knowing how to process what is coming up for you and cultivating emotional intelligence is key. Knowing how to manage your state when you do need to get something done in your business will support your growth. It is important to have emotional boundaries — not being someone that others emotionally "dump" on or doing it to others. We'll go through this in more depth later on.

WE RECEIVE FROM THE FEMININE AND GIVE FROM THE MASCULINE

To create balance, it is not one or the other. We need to be able to receive and give from a space of overflow. When you coach someone, give advice, or listen to someone, you are giving and in your masculine. In return, you need to receive—whether that's money, someone listening back, sexual pleasure, etc. When this is out of balance and you're always overworking, taking on too much responsibility, and you lack boundaries, you will be depleted.

This is why being exhausted and overworking does not help you receive more money. You would be in your masculine energy, and we receive from the feminine.

Be mindful of creating the balance. If I do a live training, I ask people to receive it, and I speak about what I love from a space of pleasure and inner guidance. At the end of a live training, I will simply take a moment to receive my breath, receive the joy of getting to deliver it, or take a walk and receive nature. Because I now am more balanced in my energy, I can feel when I am out of whack and I need to go slower or faster.

It also isn't only ease and flow—we need the action! However, when you're in balance, it comes from alignment and the feminine energy, rather than *should, have-to, or must-do*. At the beginning, as you navigate unlearning and deconditioning, you may see a pendulum swing to the polar opposite. It is important to see the edges and navigate them. We can't know the feminine energy unless we know the opposite. From there we can come into balance, and I hope with this knowledge you can stop the ongoing swinging.

The masculine doing (elements: fire and air) is powerful for getting things done, taking action, grit and creating. When it is in overdrive from a space of pushing and proving, that fire in our bodies can cause inflammation, disease and burnout. We need the balance with the feminine (elements: water and earth). I love to create balance by listening to intuitive guidance on the actions

I want to take and what I want to create. I allow myself to infuse pleasure, play, grounding, slow breathes and creativity into my work. I listen to my body when I've done too much, and I rest. When I am in masculine overdrive, I tend to feel more anger, obsession and frustration rising up. Observing these emotions and being conscious of what is happening brings me back to balance.

There has been a lot of focus on activating the divine feminine but the divine masculine is just as important. If we keep receiving guidance and not taking action, we will feel stuck, stagnant and unfulfilled.

5 WAYS TO ACTIVATE YOUR DIVINE MASCULINE

1. Follow through

When you receive intuitive guidance on your message or offers, make the commitment to follow through on it. As we follow through on what we are guided to, our intuition will strengthen and we cultivate more faith and confidence in ourselves. Even if it is something small each day, take the aligned action. Release the drama and take the action! If you're a big action taker, start to be discerning about what you're following through on. Doing it because you should, must or see others doing it gets you on the wounded side of these energies.

2. Create firm boundaries

Physical, mental, emotional and spiritual boundaries are key to remain balanced, healthy and vibrant. You can't be responsible for another human. Having firm and loving boundaries on what you are available for is key to a flourishing healthy relationships with others.

3. Radical honesty

Speaking your truth and sharing what is concerning you is important. It's not always easy, but very necessary!

4. Focus

Clarity and confidence comes from action. It is so easy to create a to-do list a mile long (that likely feels overwhelming and never gets done). As an entrepreneur, the work is never done—that is the beauty of it. On a daily basis, focus on one or two core tasks and get them done first. See an idea to completion when you receive clear guidance. Hopping from one thing to the next without finishing it is not only a waste of time, but it reduces your self-trust.

5. Cultivate routine and discipline

I used to hate routine. After leaving my corporate job, I rebelled against it. However, when I realised filling my day with things I love and started creating an empowered structure, I've been able to fit in everything I want with an overflow of time. Time expands when we value it. My work day starts at 11:00 a.m. after a long hike and personal training twice a week, and Shaun and I have one day a week just for us (no work discussed). I have calls twice a week and write my content, modules and book on the other two days. I used to do social activities during the week, but I now reserve Saturday and Sunday for friends and family. Monday is typically a flexible day to catch up with the team. Create flexibility within your routine and make it something you love—not another thing you have to do. Find joy and pleasure in the mundane. Remember, you *get* to do this.

BODY SCAN & ACTIVATION RITUAL

We can create awareness of how balanced these energies are by tuning into the body.

1. Scan your body in the mirror and then close your eyes and tune into how the left (feminine) and right (masculine) side of your body feel.
2. *What do you feel?*
3. *What do you see?*

If you find that most of your ailments—from acne to a sore shoulder—are on your left side, this may mean your feminine aspect is out of balance. If there is pain on your right side this may mean your masculine side is overtaxed. Bringing your body into balance over time by showing love, compassion and care is so important. Different areas of your body also link to specific things. For example, shoulder tension metaphysically indicates holding the weight of the world on your shoulder and taking on too much responsibility.

Journal Prompts

- What do you believe about being highly intuitive and owning your spiritual gifts? What are you not owning or passing off as "fluke"?
- What will change if you follow what you were guided to create and share?
- If you were to follow your intuition in your business and take action from this space, what would you create?
- What does a divine feminine-led business look like for you?

    E.g. Being divinely and intuitively guided and taking action from this space.

    Breaking the "rules" and connecting to the way that you desire to show up.

- If you were to show up in the balance of the divine masculine and divine feminine, what would that look like?

    E.g. I would take more action from a space of desire and pleasure.

    I would take the action I am guided to with faith.

    I would share my truth more online and know that the money will flow.

    I would get my systems and structures in place to support my feminine flow.

ALIGNING WITH YOUR MENSTRUAL CYCLE

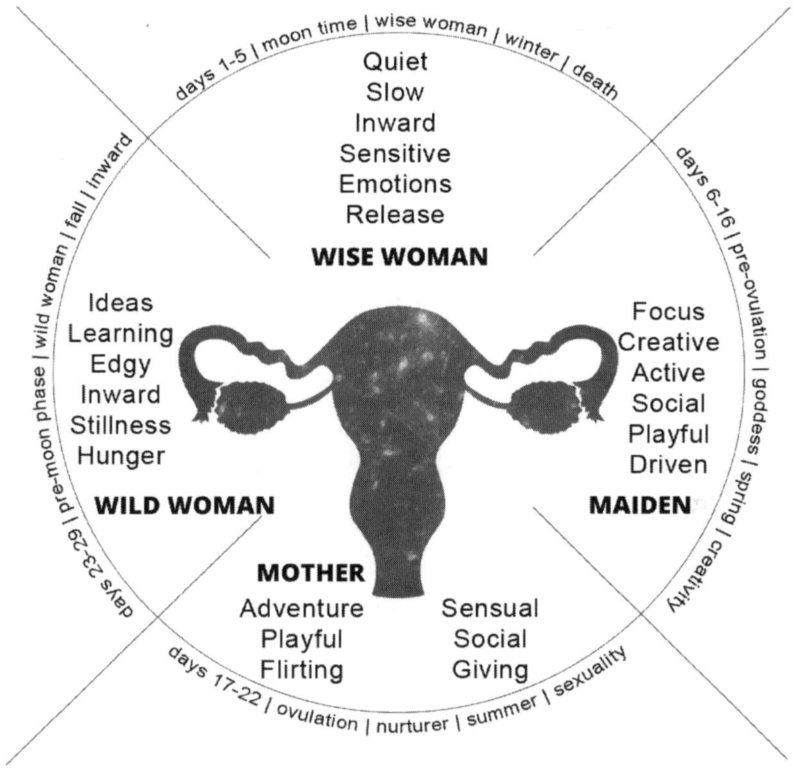

As women, it is essential to honour your menstrual cycle. In a world telling us that we need to constantly be on, *no pain no gain*, and *make it happen*, we forget to honour the natural cycle and the death and rebirth we experience every single month. For a long time, I hated my period and I dreaded that time of the month. It was no coincidence that my period was heavy and painful, irregular, and a source of frustration because I couldn't show up to work with a ton of energy. Fortunately, I started to work *with* my period, release trauma around my first period and how I viewed it, as well as run my business in alignment with my menstrual flow. If you don't have a period or it isn't regular, start to honour the natural cycles of your body and track any shifts in mood, energy and emotions during the month.

In my programs, I know when my clients have their period and when they are ovulating. I know how they see their first period and experience. I know how they see sex and pleasure.

Why? It has everything to do with creating a divine feminine-led business. We are cyclical beings and go through death and rebirth approximately every 29 days as women (it's also synced to the moon). And for women who don't menstruate—you're still connected to the cycle of the moon.

You are *not* meant to be on 24/7, 365 days a year. I see so many women judging themselves around their cycles and how they're able to show up in business. They see themselves as good when they are showing up, reaching their goals, and have high energy. But, when they are tired, emotional and don't feel like working, they are bad.

I reiterate: there is no "good," "bad," "right," or "wrong". Duality exists and our perception is what gives it meaning. When you berate and judge yourself is when your energy and vibration will dip. Honouring yourself and embracing the flow while being present for what you need to is a powerful way to expand your energetic capacity to receive.

Most women are raised in a highly masculinized world. We are raised as the "good" girl that needs to do as she is told. To truly unleash yourself and your message it is important to start to align with the natural feminine rhythms and cycles. If you aren't menstruating then starting to connect into the moon cycles is powerful.

Off of synthetic birth control, most women will sync their cycle to the New Moon, and some will sync with the Full Moon.

Honour your feminine flow and it will honour you. Here's a short summary of what you may typically feel. Start to track things in the month and really listen in.

This is a guide for a typical cycle. Make sure to start tracking how you feel daily. Monitor your energy levels, your mood, how your body feels and what you naturally feel inclined to create or write about. Make sure to give yourself rest without judging yourself during your moon time. This will allow for greater energy during the rest of the cycle. Remember, everyone is unique and it is important to track things. If you are not bleeding, then start to connect more to the moon cycles.

DAY 1 – 5: MOON TIME – BLEEDING – MENSTRUATION – WINTER

IDENTIFIED BY: Introspective, wisdom, heightened intuition, sensitive, release

This is an incredibly sacred time—celebrate it. The stillness, the shedding, the sensitivity and allowing yourself to feel what needs to be felt. It is the winter and metaphorical death.

FEMININE ARCHETYPE: Wise Woman

In Business: It is important to go inwards at this time as your body is putting the energy into shedding. Take time to shed what needs to go. Don't schedule launches, meetings or big events around this time if you can avoid it.

MESSAGING: Highly introspective and may be called to share deeper wisdom and channelled guidance. May be less inclined to want to show your face on lives or stories – allow yourself to be guided. You may desire to share the shadow self more and what has come up for you to release.

LAUNCHING: Close off the program launch before menstruation and use this time to rest so that you are ready for the next cycle. When I am well-rested in this time, the preovulatory phase is highly energised.

WAYS TO CELEBRATE:

- A beautiful bath with candles, petals or salts (whatever feels amazing for you)
- Thanking the body for this cycle
- Pouring your blood from your Mooncup back into the earth

Soul Reflection

- ▷ What am I called to share?
- ▷ What am I required to release and why is it important for my soul clients to hear this?
- ▷ What deeper questions am I receiving?
- ▷ What is my intuition guiding me to share?

RITUAL TO RELEASE

- Write out on a piece of paper everything that no longer serves you and you're reading to release, including limiting beliefs or anything you feel is holding you back.
- Burn the page.
- Cleanse your body in an Epsom salt bath and say: "I cut any chords and release (whatever you're letting go) from my energy field."
- Come back to gratitude/your intentions/guided message, or whatever is aligned to you.

RITUAL TO CELEBRATE YOUR MENSTRUAL CYCLE AND CONNECT TO YOUR FIRST PERIOD

Think back to your first period. *What happened? How did you feel?*

Put your hand on your root chakra and one hand on your heart. Hold space for that little girl as you close your eyes and visualise yourself growing from when you had your period into the wild, divine feminine women that you are now. Cry, love and embrace where needed.

DAY 6 – 16: PRE-OVULATION – SPRING

IDENTIFIED BY: Focused, confident, high energy, playful, new beginnings. Everything feels positive if you rested properly during menstruation. There is a heightened energy and sense of enthusiasm.

This is identified by more masculine energy, so you are able to tap into logic and processes here.

Feminine Archetype: Maiden

IN BUSINESS: This is the best time to start new projects! Plan speaking engagements, create your funnel, have podcast interviews, write your sales page, launch a new program.

MESSAGING: Often lighter, playful, more optimistic, I often speak about manifestation and how amazing life is, great to share the behind-the-scenes of your business and what you're birthing at this time. You may be more likely to have a lot of content you want to share and new ideas. Go with it. Batch where there is an overflow of content.

LAUNCHING: This is a great time to start your launch of your programs or create something new.

Soul Reflections

- What am I creating and excited to share?
- What is present in my life that I am grateful for?
- What can I share that is fun/playful or entertaining?

DAY 17 – 22: OVULATION – NURTURER – SUMMER

IDENTIFIED BY: Sensual, Social, Patience, ripeness, balance, creativity, inspiration, compassion, wisdom, joy.

FEMININE ARCHETYPE: Mother

If you have rested well during menstruation your energy will be high – outgoing, sensual, expressive and adventurous. If you haven't rested, feeling tired or burnout will stop you from accessing that energy that you have in this part of your cycle.

IN BUSINESS: This is a great time to launch, schedule big events and you may have energy for more calls and bigger projects.

MESSAGING: You may feel more turned on, sensual, pleasure filled. Allow yourself to tap into this divine turn on and share whatever is coming through you.

Soul Reflection

- What am I called to share?
- What would serve my audience around sensuality/sexuality/pleasure?

DAY 23 – 29: PREMENSTRUAL – WILD WOMEN – FALL/AUTUMN

IDENTIFIED BY: Wild woman, power, limitless, uninhibited, sexual, magnetic, true self.

FEMININE ARCHETYPE: Wild Woman/Priestess/Enchantress

You can trust your intuition most during this phase. With the decrease in hormones we are more likely to be expressing our true self here! The biggest shame of this phase is women are so out of balance in their energies, most waste this phase dull from Tylenol and raging from out of whack hormones. PMS is not normal. It is a symptom of disconnection from your wild nature. What I love most about this phase is that your built-in bullshit detector is heightened!

IN BUSINESS: Close carts and tie up any loose ends before resting in menstruation. Have fun and allow your wild side out! Celebrate the month and spend time doing things that turn you on.

MESSAGING: Bullshit detector, outspoken, seeing parts in society that need to be disrupted, don't take any shit, wild, and in our most connected state. This energy, when channelled, is highly magnetic. Don't dull down your true self! PMS is not something that just has to happen; it's a dulling down of our essence and truth and then we take pills to curb the lust we have, it dulls our nature. Embrace the wild, sensual and erotic woman in you.

Soul Reflection

- What do I need to share that is pissing me off?
- What am I seeing that I don't agree with?
- What do I need to share about my true and wild self?
- What do others need to know that I've been hiding about my truth?

Contrary to the messaging we're bombarded with, slowing down by choice is powerful and often requires deeper discipline than working hard. It is not weak.

Embrace Your Cycle, Integrate Shadow, And Unleash Your True Essence

When I started my business I was lost, confused and completely disconnected from my body. To be honest, I was in victim mode believing it was easy for everyone else. Despite this, I had an inner knowing that this just had to work. When I invested in Vanessa knowing I needed to be in her energy and allow more of my spiritual side to come to the surface, things changed dramatically. I started to uncover my true power, why the things that had happened to me were absolutely perfect for me, and how these were my innate gifts to help others. Working through my own shadow work, inner child healing, and clearing ancestral blocks allowed me to step fully into unleashing my full self expression.

What stopped you from believing you could be paid to be you?

I simply didn't believe I was good enough. I had a belief that I was average and that nobody would want to pay me. I just didn't know who I was because I'd spent too long perfecting masks and facades.

What was the shift that took place to get paid to be you, and how did it happen?

Choosing and deciding that I am worthy just because. That I didn't need to look outside of me anymore and everything I had was within me. It was empowering. Activating my feminine energy fully meant reclaiming my sexuality and sensuality. I found myself in a Sex Magic Ritual and later downloaded my entire soul-aligned program from this. I released years of pent-up anger and was finally able to feel safe receiving in my feminine by healing and activating this part of me. This makes it a huge part of my work now.

What would you say to someone wanting to join one of Vanessa's programs?

Do it. It will be the best investment you ever make. I have grown incredible amounts, my confidence, self-worth and self-belief. I truly don't think I would be here without Vanessa, I was so blinded by my own patterns and she has a unique gift to be able to call you out on these so quickly (with love) to help you make radical shifts.

MEGAN ROSE, Embodiment Coach
Find Megan on Instagram: @iammeganrose_

chapter 11

Your Unique Gifts & Soul Clients

You are your niche, you are your brand, you are the message, and your gifts are already within you. You get to work with whoever you want to work with, share what you want and create what you want.

As your most fully expressed and activated self, without the rules and doubt, who would you love to work with?

When I first started my business, I desired to work with corporate women who wanted to transition to entrepreneurship but didn't have the confidence to do it. I tried life coaching, health coaching, and career coaching. It all felt off. I didn't feel aligned with helping people stay in careers they hated, knowing that true freedom was beyond the cubicle (for me).

When I hired my own coach, I already knew what I wanted to do, but there were limiting beliefs stopping me from making the decision to work with corporate women who wanted to have the mindset and confidence to quit and start their own business. I soon realised that because I didn't have a 6-figure business yet and was still in a corporate job, I felt like a fraud. When I started to be transparent about where I was and that I could help with confidence, clarity and mindset for those just starting out, my business took off. I recall saying on a webinar: "I can't help you get to 6 figures because I'm not there yet, but I can help you get the confidence and clarity to start your business and not make the same mistakes as I did."

Radical honesty and integrity is sexy.

It was a profound turning point. Owning where I was and having integrity with who I wanted to work with and how I could help them. Sure, some people would have decided not to work with me, but being ashamed of my journey and not speaking my truth was far worse. In fact, it was stopping me from getting clients.

My biggest selling point was that I could help corporate clients hit 5-figure months while still working a 9-5. Had I not shared the story of returning to my corporate job, I wouldn't have had this opportunity to share. My story of going back to a corporate job, being ashamed of it, and then hitting 5 figures attracted my soul clients with ease. I understood where they were and how to get them to where they wanted to be.

The reality with coaching is you don't actually have to be a few steps ahead of your ideal client. Some of the best coaches in the world haven't achieved what they coach others on. Being a great coach is not dependent on that. You can work with whoever you want and whatever level they are at, as long as you are able to see what they need to move forward.

After burning out in 2018, the work I started to do was the alchemy between energy, mindset and strategy, so that soul clients get paid to be themselves without sacrifice.

Your soul client will evolve as you do, and the more we understand ourselves, the more we can see beliefs, fears and patterns in clients.

I believe that most marketing does this part backwards which aligns with patriarchal constructs, people-pleasing, self-sacrifice, and putting others before ourselves.

How many ideal client avatars have you done/ target market research that you've carried out that only leaves you more confused, lacking confidence, and second guessing yourself? Systems are set up to keep us further from our truth.

It is why I no longer teach this way to clients. Instead of asking what your ideal client wants, I'll ask you: *What excites you most? What do you love talking about?* Instead of asking what your ideal client will buy from you, I ask: *What are you excited to create and sell? What was missing when you were going through a particular struggle?*

You can define your niche around anything that you want. If you are a coach, healer or lightworker, your soul client and methodology will be created from your journey through pain and obstacles. It can be as narrow or as broad as you want, as long as it makes sense to *you*. You are your brand and will be magnetic when you are in your truth and sharing all parts of you, unapologetically. The more you know yourself and what you are obsessed with, the more you will magnetise your soul clients with your message.

Don't pick a niche because it is supposed to make you money or because you've been told to. Pick it because at your core, this is your purpose and mission. I see so many people trying to be business coaches because it is supposed to make money instead of doing what they are meant to and called to do. The title is irrelevant, there is no label for the multidimensional work and transformation you provide.

We always know who we are meant to work with—it is in our story, in our obsessions, in our passions, and what we speak about all the time.

Follow your desires and what turns you on. Follow what makes you feel wet, excited and alive. Like sexual energy and lust, we can use this energy in our work to magnetise clients, to activate creativity and intuition, and to spark connection.

A lot of clients come to me with issues with clarity on discovering who is their soul client. They've been going around in circles with who they are meant to serve. This is deeply rooted in fears, and often not a clarity issue.

COMMON FEARS I SEE IN MY CLIENTS

1. Fear of rejection

Sometimes masking this with "I need more clarity" or "I don't know enough yet" Having potential clients say no is part of this process, and has nothing to do with your self-worth or being enough. It simply means that those people are not your soul clients. Your soul clients will be excited to pay you. You can't do anything wrong with soul clients other than not show up fully or not speak your truth.

2. Fear of not being good enough

You do something really well and you enjoy doing it, but deep down you wonder why someone would pay you for it. But the thing that you feel is not enough is often your unique gift. Your superpowers are meant to feel easy and amazing and come naturally to you. If it feels effortless and you see something that is unique for you, embrace that magic.

▷ What feels so easy and comes naturally to me that I don't feel I could charge for?

3. Trying to please everyone

When we try to speak to everyone, we end up speaking to no one. Don't worry about leaving people out. Focus on attracting your soul clients and being unapologetically you. The uncomfortable parts you're afraid to share—those are what you're meant to be sharing and will create the greatest impact and attract clients to you.

Your gifts and your magic are often hidden in your trauma, beliefs and childhood. Go to them, lean into what they are telling you and allow yourself to release them.

OWNING YOUR INNER POWER

"Our deepest fear is that we are powerful beyond measure. It is our light, not our darkness, that most frightens us."

—MARIANNE WILLIAMSON

As someone who spent most of their life giving their power away to something external, it feels incredible to have true inner peace. To know that I am infinitely taken care of, and that everything in my life has happened for me, not to me. That I am, like you, made for more.

You were not born to be like anyone else—you were born to lead, to rise, and to shift the paradigm. You are *you*, which is perfect. You are not meant to be like anyone else online. Just like your thumb print, you are original and unique. There is no comparison and in fact, if you try to compare yourself to others or wish you had what they have, you'll move further from your truth and essence.

You are a perfect, divine creation with everything you need right now to create success on your terms. You need to remember the miracle you are and just how perfect you already are. You are not like anyone else. That is your superpower.

What if you remembered your power and the gifts that were bestowed upon you at birth?

What if you stopped fighting yourself and embraced the magic that resides in every cell of your being?

It's time to return home to the lost world within you. Where ancient wisdom, love and confidence was buried.

It's time to return home to you and remember who you are. The divine gifts you have and the magic and lust for life that you have forgotten.

What if today was the day that you forgave, that you released, and that you remembered?

Your light may scare you. Your power and resilience may baffle you. Those around you wonder how you do what you do.

You've been dulling down and dimming your light your whole life. Afraid to disrupt, disturb and be too much.

Your greatest gift is in what you're afraid to be, dear visionary. Your gift is you being your bold, courageous and incredible self. The gift to the world and the key to unlocking your purpose, soul's calling and destiny is calling back and owning all parts of you.

This life that you've been given is a gift. It's time to use your voice and unique gifts in the way they are meant to. No more hiding or watering down your magnificence.

It's time to be bold, to speak your truth, and to create an incredible ripple effect of change in the world.

No one else has your story.

No one has your unique combination of gifts.

No one has the journey, heartache and pain that you've experienced.

There is no competition when you own your uniqueness and show up in your truth.

If this is the only thing you take from this book, remember: **you were born perfect with a soul's purpose.** You incarnated in this lifetime as a template of perfection with unique gifts, soul contracts and challenges. There is no coincidence that you are doing the work you are called to do and that you were born at this particular point in history. Yes, you are here to create a ripple effect of change in the lives of others and shift the consciousness of the planet with your work. The way you've viewed perfection has been distorted through conditioning, ancestral patterns and society.

Perfection is not an airbrushed model you see, the Instagram-perfect lifestyle, or whatever you view as "perfect" or separate from you. Right now as you sit reading this, you are more than enough.

Embrace just how perfect you are. When you realise that you are a miracle and whole already, you are able to truly make the impact you are meant to. Remember, everything is happening for your growth and evolution. We go through particular struggles to be able to help others with similar wounds. I say that burnout was my greatest gift and lesson, and now that I have healed and am thriving, I can help others overcome this.

Soul Reflection

- What do others keep telling me I'm amazing at?
- What do I love in my career?

- ▷ What have I studied or read about that I loved?
- ▷ What do most clients say I'm amazing at supporting them with?
- ▷ What comes naturally to me?
- ▷ What traumatic parts of my life have blocked certain gifts, skills and knowledge? What do I need to bring back?
- ▷ What are my spiritual gifts? How do I uniquely see things?

  (Clairvoyance means clear seeing, Clairaudience means clear hearing, Clairsentience means clear feeling, Clairalience means clear smelling, Clairgustance means clear tasting, and Claircognizance means clear knowing.)
- ▷ How do these spiritual gifts support my soul clients?
- ▷ What have I learned about my gifts, skills and knowledge?

YOUR SELF WORTH

You were born worthy and you will die worthy. The amount of money you make, the results of your clients, the goals you reach, how many push-ups you can do, or the abs you can or can't see do not determine your worth.

One of my greatest lessons has been detaching my self-worth from client results and what I make in my business. It is no coincidence that the more worthy you feel without anything external, the more life shows up in ways to mirror that. It starts with you deeply owning your brilliance and who you are without waiting for something to show up in your reality to tell you you are worthy.

If everything that you thought determined your worthiness—money, your home, your car, the clients—was gone, who would you be?

When I was suicidal, I thought that if I lost the business and all my money, that the only option was to end my life. That I was worthless without them.

Instead, I found myself and I came into soul alignment. If everything was taken away tomorrow, I know I would be able to rebuild and recreate everything because I have me, I have my gifts, and I have a burning passion and lust for life. When you know that you can survive losing it all, you know you can survive anything.

Journal Prompts

- Who are you without the things that you thought were your identity?
- What would you now create in your life if you built everything from truth and joy?

DEVOTION AND OBSESSION TO YOUR LIFE'S WORK

Do you believe that you shouldn't really enjoy your work? Perhaps it has been deeply ingrained in you that work should be hard and life can only be enjoyed when you retire.

I felt this for a long time! I felt guilty truly loving what I do and felt strange saying how much I love my work when those around me were complaining about theirs. Give yourself full permission to love your work and to design your business around your life and what you desire.

Allow yourself to fall in love with your obsession, your devotion, your passion, and the richness of the tapestry of who you are.

Most of the clients I work with have a mission, a message, and a deep desire to be seen in a *big way*. But wanting to be seen, be heard, and be the centre of attention is often seen as too much or too loud.

Today, I want you to let that all go. There is a reason that you desire what you desire and a reason that you are called to stand up and be heard. You have an important message that the world needs to hear. It is time for them to hear it. You can't want to be seen deep down, and then hide your truth and essence. Radical and brutal honesty will set you free.

YOUR STORY AND SIGNATURE OFFER

I thought that my story wasn't enough. Have you ever felt this way? It is nothing to be ashamed of—most of the clients I work with come to me thinking that their story is boring or they don't have anything mind blowing to share.

Most of them think that their story isn't enough, because they think *they* aren't enough. Of course, we can shift that.

If you don't have a rags-to-riches story or a massive shift in income or major wins, no one will want to listen, right? This is not the truth.

Your story has the power to change, shift and heal those around you in a way that only you can tell it. The pain, the struggles, and the way you create your life and business is something to be applauded.

There I was, hiring an incredible publicist and at the same time, I was doubting my message. We were trying to arrange a TEDx Talk, and I was afraid of what I would speak about. *Like really afraid.*

I remember a friend asking me what I would say, and I answered: "You know, stuff. Lots of stuff that has happened!" I didn't have a clue.

Even at that stage of my journey, I had a lot to share but I wasn't truly owning any part of it.

YOUR SIGNATURE OFFER RITUAL

Connect to your story and write a letter to yourself outlining your key struggles, what you had to do to overcome those struggles, what it felt like to overcome them, and what resources you wished you could have had available to you then. Be specific and concise.

- ▷ What parts of your journey would you love to help someone with? Your signature offer and the struggles that you've overcome is a great way to uncover your signature offer(s).
- ▷ What parts feel uncomfortable to support someone with? Why does it feel uncomfortable?
- ▷ What have you learned?

CLIENT RESULTS AND ENERGY

I used to have sleepless nights over client results. I would often wake up in a panic and check in on my clients. Not only is this unhealthy for your nervous system, it undermines the magnificence and resourcefulness of the incredible people you're working with.

You are not here to fix or save another person (we often do this because of not feeling good enough, and it serves us). Believing that your clients are broken, or that you're more powerful than them, does *not* serve them.

They are incredible, magical, and absolutely divine. Speak to their magnificence and higher self instead of attaching your self-worth to their results. When I started to protect my energy, raise my vibration, and allow my clients to entrain their energy to me, the transformations with clients became even more profound. They are creating a change, you are a mirror and guide for their expansion.

The **Law of Entrainment** states when two different frequencies are in the presence of one another, they will always come into resonance with each other; the lower frequency will move up to meet the higher one.

Allow them to come to you. The magic is only possible if you remove the ego and know that your self-worth isn't attached to the outcome.

No More Hiding

What is your story and journey to being paid to be you?

When I started working with Vanessa, I was a few months out of leaving my corporate job. I had 13 years of experience from Coaching in Corporate, to working in HR, and studying Psychology and Positive Psychology, Mindfulness and much more. However, with all of this experience I was frustrated and massively dulling my light.

I had worked with a business coach before who told me to calm down and just work on one thing. So when I left my corporate job, all I did was sell my Mindfulness courses at a low price. There were huge parts of me I was not sharing, including my spiritual awakening, which until I worked with Vanessa I believed was something I just dabbled with behind closed doors.

I also had really quite low self-esteem and because I had been in burnout, I was too scared to actually allow clients to come in, which was something I wasn't consciously aware of. Vanessa worked with my mindset and beliefs around this and we discovered the low self-esteem issue was due to bullying that had happened when I was 10. We worked through this with kinetic shift and coaching, which was amazing.

Coaching with Vanessa changed my business and my life. . I felt empowered and positive that I could share all parts of me with my audience, and I attracted amazing clients into my space who resonated with that version of me. No more hiding! Vanessa and I worked together to download my Shine Academy program, which has seen great results with clients and means I have the ability to scale my business as well as including all my incredible skills I've built up over the last 13 years.

What stopped you from believing you could be paid to be you?

I had low self-esteem, I thought everyone else was better than me, and that version of me didn't deserve to be paid to be me. I also just didn't have the awareness as I was 'told' by certain business coaches I had to follow certain rules and I had to push through things that I hated. The more I pushed, the less my business progressed.

What was the shift that took place to get paid to be you, and how did it happen?

Integrating ALL parts of me: knowing it was safe to share my whole journey and spiritual awakening with my audience. This helped me to find my people. Clearing away blocks that were holding me back, with the support and challenge of Vanessa stepping up into that higher version of myself.

What would you say to someone wanting to join one of my programs?

Do not hesitate-- it won't just change your business, it will change your life.

GEMMA SANDWELL

www.thehappinessbranch.com

chapter 12

Magnetic Messaging & Vibrational Marketing

You have a reason for being, a purpose, and a message within you that needs to be shared with the world.

I don't write content to convert—I know my content will magnetise my soul clients because I confidently share what I am guided to share. It converts because I believe it does.

All I'm required to do is show up, speak my truth, and be of service in the world. Soul clients are magnetised to me with ease. I do, however, confidently share my programs and how to connect with me almost every day. We are doing a disservice to ourselves and our audience by withholding our gifts.

Vibrational Marketing reminds us that your soul clients are already in your vortex ready to pay you. You have soul agreements with them. Your marketing is not about getting people to find you, being on a million platforms, or doing more. It is about getting you into the vortex with belief, turn-on, and excitement.

When you are lit up and sharing what you are called to, you are a magnet for soul clients.

Often, we find ourselves so caught up in comparison and the rules, that we move far away from our voice and tone.

YOU GO FIRST, AND SOUL CLIENTS WILL FOLLOW

We are blessed with being fortunate enough to be born in a time where we can speak our truth, share our message and our medicine, and not be burnt at the stake for it!

Your community is looking to you to go first, to rise up, and to lead. When you go first, soul clients will naturally be drawn to you.

The energy of an unapologetic woman on the rise is magnetic!

It is important to cultivate a firm belief that your message matters. Belief and your energy are the cornerstone of what you write.

5 WAYS TO AMPLIFY YOUR MESSAGE

1. Speaking your truth

Tell the truth everywhere you can. Radical honesty in all areas of your life will shift everything.

I remember working with a client who was getting irritated with her partner. To try and keep the peace, she was skirting around the edges and not fully honouring herself or her business. She was trying to please and accommodate him, which only created a greater rift in their relationship.

She has recently gotten married, after wondering whether the relationship would continue. She sent me this message: "Radical honesty transformed everything."

So much of the modelling that we've seen for intimate relationships (or even for interpersonal relationships in general) in our culture encourages dishonesty. "White lies are fine," to not hurt someone's feelings. Or worse: "Don't ask, don't tell." This will always come back to bite you, or you'll continue to feel shame, resent and guilt.

Speaking your truth extends to your social media, your programs, and with your clients. If you would tell a best friend, tell your clients and followers.

The best advice I received about speaking my truth online was: "If you are doing something with a client, but not sharing it online, you'll end up attracting people that aren't aligned or ready for your work."

I don't believe in giving anyone what they want, and not what they need. As someone put it: "Give the chocolate not the broccoli." I disagree. If you're helping clients deal with trauma, tell them. If you're supporting clients with energy healing, tell them. If you're helping clients with emotional release, tell them. If you're helping clients with Facebook ads and funnels, tell them.

Don't hide or withhold any part of you—it just makes things harder.

Put your hand on your heart and say this prayer with me:

Use me in the way you see best. May the message that is meant to be shared for my highest good and the highest good of humanity—come to me with ease. Let the Grace of the Universe move through me to shine a light for those that are ready for it. May my message touch and impact the lives of those that need to hear it today. I surrender and trust that my message is more than enough.

This has been something that many struggle with. For a long time, I struggled to be radically honest and show all of myself because of old conditioning, patterns and habits. I thought that vulnerability was weak, because I associated vulnerability with crying. Of course, my conditioning taught me that crying was bad.

The truth: **vulnerability is courage.** Showing all parts of you, in your wholeness, by integrating the light and shadow, will set you free.

The more unapologetically you show up online, the more magnetic you will be. The more you speak your truth in life, the more you honour who you are as a person, the more your energy and frequency will increase. Radical honesty with others and yourself will set you free.

What does that mean to really speak your truth? It seems so elusive, so easy, and yet so difficult all at the same time.

Remember: your truth is *you.* It's the things you think, it's the things you have been ashamed of, the things you find funny or sad, the things that make you angry, the struggles and pain in your heart. The thoughts you have behind closed doors. The things you want to say to family, friends or neighbours but often don't because of fear of judgment, not being liked, or fear of conflict.

Soul Reflection

- What do I know I stand for/against?
- What am I hiding that my soul client needs to hear?
- What am I ashamed of that my soul client needs to hear?
- What would I share with myself, in my relationships, and with my community if I released the fears and stopped caring how others would take it (which is always self-protection anyway)?
- What areas of my life and business am I not showing radical honesty?

Over the next few days, pay attention to *anything* and everything that causes an emotional charge, any sort of trigger/upset/rant/excitement/fun/adventure/craziness/sadness etc. Think about what you would most likely message your best friend about, and use it in your content.

Remember, your best marketing and selling is sharing *you*—and *you* are not a concept. It's what is happening right now, moment to moment.

I've always found that what I am going through and elicits a response within me is what resonates most with my audience.

Don't filter yourself—whatever comes through, share it and link it back to what you're selling.

It's fun! My best content is written when I share something I've been hiding or ashamed of, or something I think might be unpopular.

2. Calling back your power

For the past few years, I have been learning about Gene Keys and Human Design. I don't know how many times I have read or heard that I am magnetic, brilliant, and that I can create whatever I want.

But there I was, scrolling the internet for another course and asking *yet again* for validation. I said: "I want to do more shadow work, trauma release, and nervous system healing." I already had all of these tools and qualifications. I didn't need another course showing me another way to do it.

I've had my fair share of moments where I didn't think I was good enough to do the work I do… despite having thousands of testimonials that say otherwise. *For f**k sakes, how many more testimonials do you need to feel good enough?* The reality is, it would never be enough.

Unless you say f**k it.

Unless you own and claim that you're brilliant, a genius, and a badass leader.

This isn't unique for me: *you* are magnificent.

There isn't one client that has come into my programs that isn't powerful, incredible, divine, unstoppable, and limitless. You have the power within you *right now* to create whatever you want. It's just depends on how long it takes you to say: "F**k it, I am powerful, I own my uniqueness."

You don't need more testimonials or more qualifications—you need to own your power. You don't need to be like Sally down the road. You need to be more *you*. When you come home to your truth, remember who you are, stop thinking that you need someone outside of you to fix, save or heal you—*that* is when you own your power.

No one else can save you! I've tried that. We can't bypass discomfort. The only healing is self-healing. Stop trying to protect old wounds and hang on to the past so that you can play safe. You don't have to go to hypnotherapy, ancestral healing, then counselling. (Sometimes it's really fun to be trying out all sorts of things to actually avoid your truth.) Get support with one person and show up for it fully. I love all those modalities, but moving from one to the next trying to find *the thing* isn't necessarily serving you. *The thing* has been there all along. It's you.

If you have a block that you're consciously aware of, it's no longer a block—it's a choice. On some level, it's safer to hold on to it and you're avoiding the discomfort of what the next level will require of you.

- ▷ Why is it not safe?
- ▷ Why is it safe? What needs to be released?

Hiring a new team member is scary. Letting go of an old program that makes money is scary. Letting go of a money block so that you need to charge more and quit your corporate job is scary. Owning your power *is* uncomfortable.

It means admitting to being good enough in a world bombarding us with messages telling us we need to be more, do more, and have more.

Everything we see tells us we are not good enough. To give yourself a compliment is frowned upon or seen as bragging. I say, shout it out and own it, which means you're going to need to step up and take the aligned action required for the big, bold vision that you say you want.

You are deeply guided. No more excuses. It's vulnerable. It's scary. It's uncomfortable.

But you know what's worse? Staying in the same space.

You have everything you need within you. It is time to rise up, lead, and create a powerful movement with your message.

Remember: being in your power is not forceful, manipulative, or aggressive. To be in your power is to be in alignment. To be in your power is to trust that you are in the right place at the right time. It is about owning all parts of you and confidently pursuing what you're destined for.

3. Cultivating belief and confidence

Your soul clients are waiting and ready to pay you whatever you charge. Marketing is not about doing things to get in front of your audience—it's about you getting into belief and confidence around your offer and shouting it out in a way that feels most aligned. Sales is a transference of belief. Soul clients buy into your energy.

When you walk into a room, people sense your aura before they see you. Online is the same— your energy doesn't lie.

The other part is trusting that the message you are being guided to share is more than enough. You don't have to have templates or a guide on creating content. There is no template for the message of your soul, but depending on where you are in your journey, you may need some masculine structures.

If you've had worthiness issues and beliefs that you're not good enough (most of us do in some capacity), you may think it has to be more complicated than this. It isn't! your message is you— it is what you love to share, what you're passionate about, your fears, and guilty pleasures.

It is the totality of your being. You will never run out of content by sharing what is on your mind.

Repeat after me: my message is more than enough. I'm worthy of being seen and heard. My message has the potential to impact lives and shift the paradigm by being me.

When you're expressing yourself and giving your gifts to the world, when you really show up in your life, when you put yourself out there...the Universe responds in kind.

It rewards you.

Energy comes back to you in the form of abundance, wealth, and all the things your heart desires.

It's the great Universal exchange.

The more you get in touch with your sensual energy, which is your creative blueprint—remember, all of your entire genetic code is housed here—you get more in touch with your true self.

Your work becomes more of an extension of you.

You self-realise in all parts of your life.

Journal Prompts

Take some time to answer the following questions, and get into your beliefs. Release the rules.

- What are the 50 reasons why your program is life-changing? (I keep this in the front of my journal.)
- What do you feel about your pricing? Is it too high or too low? If it's too high, how can you close the gap and feel more confident in the pricing ? If it is too low, what do you need to increase it to?
- You already are at your next level. What are the thoughts, words, energy and actions if you already had your vision? How can you collapse timelines and show up like this now?
- If you fully embodied that version of you and made creating whatever you desired easy, how would you show up, what would you wear, and how would you interact?
- What rules and regulations have you created for self around messaging?
- If you gave yourself full permission to create and write with fun and pleasure, what would you do?

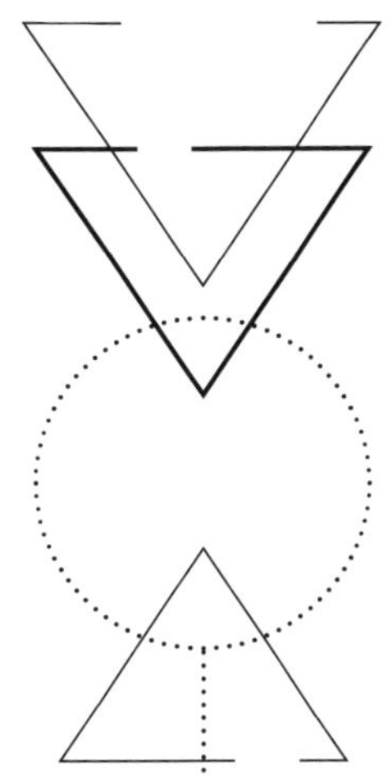

Repeat after me: My message has the potential to impact lives and shift the paradigm by being me.

4. Activating your intuition and downloading your message

If you are doing your soul's work and fulfilling your divine assignment on this planet, you will be a channel and messenger for the divine.

It is time to start allowing the message to channel through you. Most of us are disconnected from our nature, our feminine wildness, and source energy—start to reconnect.

▷ How do you channel your message? Is it in meditation? Walking in nature? Taking a shower? Think about times where you get that deep inner knowing, that feeling that is unique to you, that just feels right.

Remember: you don't have to do anything to channel your message or programs. You are the messenger, you have a divine inner intelligence and higher self. Being intuitive and divinely guided is not reserved for "those other people." If you slow down enough to hear, you can channel. Everyone can. If you're not already being guided on your message or program, practice this exercise and start to get even more curious:

- **SET THE INTENTION**

  Set the intention to release the should, have-to, must-do, or fear of judgement.

  You can use the prayer above, or:

  Angels, spirit and guardians of the highest truth and order, please support me with sharing the message I am born to. Allow me to channel from the divine, the message that is meant to be shared.

- **DISCONNECT TO RECONNECT**

  Go for a walk, dance, shower, meditate or have a bath. Disconnect from social media and your phone. Allow yourself to be completely disconnected from the busyness of life, be silent, and with yourself. Drop into your body and out of your head as you allow yourself to reconnect to your inner voice.

  Nature is incredibly healing and nurturing. Starting to reconnect to mother earth is such an important part of coming back to your innate ability to be intuitive, guided and at peace. The whole Universe is working through you as you align to the rhythms and cycles—how can you ever doubt your magic or that of being a divine creation?

- **OBSERVE AND JOURNAL**

  Observe what is coming through you. Take notes, write without thinking, and allow what needs to come through, come through. Be divinely present in the moment.

▷ What am I being guided to share?

▷ What is coming through at this moment?

- **TRUST YOUR GUT**

  Start to share whatever is coming through you without fear of judgement from others or yourself. Trust that your message is important, needs to be shared, and that you will be guided with writing and sharing it. It wouldn't be there if it wasn't important!

- **HONOUR YOUR INNER INTELLIGENCE, ENERGY AND EMOTIONS**

If anything comes up, observe it, connect to it, and identify with your truth. If fears come up or it feels uncomfortable, feel it, especially if it is part of your shadow self, something you're ashamed of, or something you've been suppressing. Why would you be receiving this guidance and message if you were not meant to share it?

Ask yourself:

▷ Why is this important for my soul clients to hear? How will this set me free?

Listen into how your body responds—excitement, joy, pleasure, turn-on, discomfort, fear, sadness. Anything that evokes an emotion within you will evoke emotions and deep connection within your clients.

Fall in love with the process of writing, being on video, and sharing your message with the world. It gets to be fun, pleasurable, and deliciously uncomfortable.

Remember: that rush of adrenaline, turn-on, and adventure when you post something that scares you is *amazing*. You have the option: you can be safe and dull with your content, or you can alchemise and transmute your struggles into beautiful content that shifts your audience. It's your choice!

5. Focus on connection

Often, we get so caught up in *more*. More people viewing our stories, bigger lists, more platforms, and more people in groups.

More is not necessarily better, and the random statistics about how many people need to show up to your training or download your free content really aren't supported. I prefer to focus every day on how I can create a better connection with my audience *today*. That may mean sharing something vulnerable, it may be commenting on a post or reaching out to thank someone for being in my group. Build genuine human connections with real care. Those that are in your community are there for a reason. Try not to judge your community. Open your heart to love and care.

Our deepest need is to be seen. We crave connection and safety. Allow your audience to be fully seen, heard, and understood through your content.

Journal Prompts

- How can you create more intimacy with those souls already in your community?
- What makes you feel valued, heard and loved in a community? How can you create this?

I'm not saying go overboard with connecting to everyone frantically. Stand in your power and worthiness, and be social.

How Aneta Became A Magnet For Soul Clients

I remember exactly how I felt when I first saw Vanessa`s post on Instagram. I didn't believe that a freedom lifestyle and being a successful online coach was possible for me. I was stuck in comparison, procrastinating on taking any action towards building my dream. I was the queen of excuses: my kids, my accent, even my braces – they all prevented me from showing up. Yet, one day I decided to book that call with Vanessa after reading some of her content.

That call changed my entire life.

I still remember that energy. I knew I had to get into her program and I said `yes` without looking at her sales page. To be honest, I had no idea which program I was signing up to. But one thing was certain – things were going to start happening for me. I felt it. No more excuses.

Thanks to being in Vanessa`s Mastermind program, Supercharge Your Success, I understood I get to be paid for being me. I started honouring myself and stepped into the woman I came here to be. I fell in love with my life & started manifesting all my desires with ease.

I became the most unapologetic and magnetic version of me.

My business exploded, I created my signature program, I started magnetizing soul clients through my content. Even after Supercharge, I have continued to work with Vanessa in her membership, Wild, Bold & Free and thanks to her powerful breathwork sessions my vision gets clearer all the time. Having Vanessa's support & access to her precious energy is priceless.

ANETA GÓRECKA is a Business Coach helping women coaches and entrepreneurs create freedom based businesses through mindset, marketing & magnetism.

Find Aneta on Instagram:
www.instagram.com/anetabizcoach

Thank you for journeying with me through these pages, activations, and stories. I am grateful for you. I am grateful that you have chosen to release old conditioning so that you can be a light in the world.

When you rise up and own your brilliance, you give others permission to do the same.

Embody the activation from these pages, embrace your magnificence, and go into the world creating the ripple effect of change you are born for.

You are worthy as you are.

You are loved as you are.

Having it all is your birthright.

With so much love,

Vanessa xox

CITATIONS

Jenny Rogers. Coaching Skills: The definitive guide to being a coach, Fourth Edition (England: McGraw-Hill Education, 2016)

Stephen W. Porges, The Polyvagal Theory: The Transformative Power of Feeling Safe (New York: WW Norton & Company Inc. 2017)

Peter A. Levine, Phd. Trauma and Memory: Brain and Body in the search for the living Past. (California, North Atlantic Books, 2015)

Judith Corvin-Blackburn. Activating Your 5D Frequency: A Guidebook for the journey into Higher Dimensions (Vermont: Bear & Company, 2020)

Debbie Ford, Deepak Chopra and Marianne Williamson. The Shadow Effect: Illuminating the Power of your True Self (New York: HarperCollins, 2010)

Dr Joe Dispenza. Breaking The Habit of Being Yourself. (United States: Hay House, Inc. 2017)

ABOUT THE AUTHOR

Vanessa Hallick is a world-renowned Mindset and Intuitive Business coach and founder of the Rapid Energetic Recoding™ Method. She is obsessed with helping visionary entrepreneurs create a freedom-based business, using savvy strategies and soul alignment...all while having fun!

She empowers you to be the best version of yourself and create your definition of success while being abundant, confident and happy. Her mission is to support you in creating your richest and most exciting reality, by helping you achieve your big goals without feeling overwhelmed.

Vanessa went from being fired from her sales job in recruitment to building a business that has generated millions of dollars (without a sales team) and has helped thousands of entrepreneurs shift their mindset, speak their truth, and grow their business *without sacrifice.* She loves supporting clients with the process of selling and sees it as a powerful portal for change. She believes more money in the hands of goodhearted women can do great things!

Her work has been featured in *Forbes, Red Online, Financial Times, Irish Examiner,* and other publications.

After packing up their London life, her soulmate Shaun quit his corporate finance role and joined the company as partner and CFO. Together they moved to Bali for 2.5 years and travelled all around South East Asia.

They now live in Vanessa's hometown in Knysna, South Africa where she will frequently be found walking in the local forest with Apollo, their golden retriever, sharing her daily inspiration on Instagram.

Together, they've created their version of success and freedom. A life on their terms by their own design. Vanessa is truly grateful to be able to spread her message further and impact millions, make millions, and give back freely to causes close to our heart.

ACKNOWLEDGEMENTS

Writing this part really, shows how much support is needed to write a book and the guidance and love of so many people.

Thank you, I love you.

Shaun, thank you for supporting me through this process of writing the book. Celebrating me and reminding me of my brilliance. When I doubted myself, you told me I could do it. When I wondered if anyone would want to read it—you told me how it would change the lives of those that needed it, and would be wildly successful. Thank you for believing in me and holding me to my highest self.

To my mom, Janet, for teaching me that anything is possible, to think outside the box, and to always honour my uniqueness. You instilled in me a belief that I could do anything and for that I am eternally grateful. Thanks for loving me, supporting me, and showing me the areas where I can grow. Thanks for giving me life. I love our long conversations around spirituality and consciousness. Love you, mom.

To my Dad, Derek, for loving his kids fiercely. I know that you would do anything for us and I'm so grateful. I'm grateful for all the lessons and gifts you have given me. There are a lot of great memories to cherish. Without my childhood, I wouldn't be who I am today and for that I am fortunate. Thanks for believing in me and being proud of me, even when most of what I do feels foreign to you! You instilled in me a go getter attitude and the resilience and grit to deal with any circumstances. Thank you, I love you.

My siblings Michael, Jenée and Sean Hallick. You are all so different, so magical, and so wild. I don't know what life would be like without you. I wish we all lived closer to each other! Although I had a lot of hand-me-downs and I didn't always get the second helpings of food

I wanted, I wouldn't change the memories and the fun we had and continue to have for anything. You've triggered me, you've challenged me, you've made me laugh until I cry and you've supported me. The awesome Hallick four!

To my nieces and nephews, Nicholas Hallick, Julia Hallick, Bianca Hallick, Jordan Hallick, Braden Hallick and Jaxon Hallick you light up my world. The play, the joy and the wonder. I wish you all lived closer but know that I love you so much and am proud of each one of you. Live life beyond limits, enjoy every moment and do more of what makes you happy. You are gifted.

To my dear extended family, Craig Dale, Jen Dale, Tammeré Ann Hallick, Rochelle Folkard Torres, Carol Pollock, Daria Bielerzewska *and Ale* Espinola. *Thank you for all of your support, joy, love and laughter. I truly appreciate the kind words, the enthusiasm, and how you have all been there for me opening your hearts and homes.*

To Kama Berman, a special friend who continues to be a mirror for my deepest truths and evolution. Through years apart and oceans between us, she continues to support me, love me and evolve with me. I am so grateful to have you close by and in my life.

To friends and family, thank you for supporting me and never doubting me. Thank you for your role that you've played in my life, the lessons you continue to teach me, and the wisdom that you impart. Thanks for your understanding when I've turned down social events for work and writing. I appreciate the triggers and the opportunity for me to see myself fully through you.

Ashley-Ann, without you this book wouldn't have happened. You lovingly guided me through each step of the process of writing the book, finding the right support for editing, publishing and design. You helped me feel confident and believe in getting it out there. Thank you.

Emily Dickinson, thank you for the hours spent editing the book, making it read better, and for cheering me on along the way with your encouragement. As the second person to read the book, it felt deeply vulnerable and scary to share it. I appreciate you for shifting things and providing feedback in a way that supported my own growth.

My clients and past clients, without you I wouldn't have the business and lessons in business that I have to write this book. Each day, I feel incredibly grateful to do work I love with the most amazing women in the world. Thank you for trusting in me, teaching me so much and for supporting my bigger vision and mission. I appreciate every one of you.

To Kylie Nel, Christy Cegelski, Aneta Górecka, Talea Pattemore, Jess Rowe, Victoria Bond, Patricia Auer, Leanna Glazier Hunt, Cortney Johnson, Gemma Sandwell and Megan Rose, thank you for sharing your Paid To Be You story and showing others what is possible for them. Your work and commitment to creating a ripple effect of change in the world is powerful to witness. The women you are and the role models & leaders you've stepped into is something to be celebrated. Thank you.

To my Mentors, Coaches, Teachers and Energy Healers that have supported me and been there to guide me and be a mirror for my expansion. There are so many to name, but I am grateful for the part that each one of you played in this book and helping me step into who I am today.

To Colleen Van Heerden, for the Reiki attunements, the unwavering support after burnout, the love and for listening, guiding and teaching me. I am forever grateful for your support.

To my incredible support team Claire Wescombe, Chantal Gatien and everyone at The Studio Press, thank you so much for your help, guidance and excitement with the book and my bigger mission and vision. I appreciate you so much and excited for everything else we will create together.

To Shawna Poliziani at Wolves and Roses Creative, thank you for the incredible cover design and truly capturing the essence of the book and what it represents.

To Apollo, our beautiful golden retriever. Guides, activators and healers come in all shapes and forms. Thank you for the countless walks in the forest receiving guidance for the book and the many mornings and evenings under my desk keeping me company. You truly are a blessing in our lives bringing so much joy, playfulness and a ton of crazy!

To Karin Chan Makeup and Sharyn Hodges Photography—thank you so much for the incredible photoshoot for the book. After a few shoots rescheduled due to weather, we captured the most amazing photo. I appreciate both of you for the laughter, swearing, encouragement and all the jokes, it made it such a fun experience. You went over and above to capture me in my essence.

To each and every one of you that has purchased the book, thank you so much for being here and for being willing to do the deeper work. Wishing you an overflow of abundance in all areas of your life. You truly do get Paid To Be You!

RESOURCES

Programs

PAID TO BE YOU ACADEMY

Paid To be You is an 12 module program that walks you through this book in depth. It provides videos, training, activations and workbooks filled with additional information to implement and embody the work you've done. If you're ready to take what you've learnt to the next level and elevate your income, impact and intimacy, this is for you!

www.vanessahallick.com/ptbyacademy

PAID TO BE YOU CERTIFICATION

The only certification that combines the tools to understand yourself at the deepest level, unlock your sales & money codes and support your clients with Rapid Energetic Recoding™ and mind blowing transformations

Some programs teach sales, some money, some embodiment and some mindset and then some how to create client transformations. Not around here. We believe that you are multifaceted and for true rapid shifts , you need all of these (without feeling overwhelmed and doing 10 million certifications)

We will teach you Vanessa's signature Rapid Energetic Recoding ™ Method , Facilitating Breathwork for Business, how to create a powerful activation for your clients and Unlock Their Signature Offer & Methodology (or your own).

www.vanessahallick.com/ptbycertification

SUPERCHARGE YOUR SUCCESS BY DESIGN

A 3 or 6 month mastermind for visionary women on a mission to create wealth, impact and purpose in alignment with their Human Design. A 16 module program taking you through the Mindset, Energy and Marketing required to build a sustainable multiple — 6 figure business without sacrifice. It is a space for you, if you're ready to have it all on your terms and you're ready to take the aligned action on behalf of your bigger vision.

www.vanessahallick.com/sysbd

ELEVATE BY DESIGN

A 6 month mastermind for big dreams and visionary 6 figure business owners ready to scale to 7 figures (and beyond). This is for you if you're ready to amplify your message, build your team and create scalable offers you love and that get results. We look at your signature 7 figure blueprint for success and through upleveling your mindset, uncovering your unique genius and helping you build a team that supports your bigger vision you dial up abundance in all areas of your life. As a savvy CEO of an empire, it is essential to take care of it's most important asset, you. It's time to create more spaciousness, support and leadership to leave your legacy and create the impact you were born for.

www.vanessahallick.com/elevate-your-success

WILD, BOLD & FREE MEMBERSHIP

The Wild, Bold & Free Society is a monthly membership for Visionary entrepreneurs ready to live a soul-led life and to create a business by design so that you can be a magnet for wealth, health and happiness. You'll receive trainings, journal prompts & visualisations on Mindset, Energy and Marketing. There are monthly Revelation Breathwork sessions to receive guidance on your intentions in your business so that you feel calm, confident and clear on the next steps to take to build your empire. You'll be surrounded by a high vibrational group of women on a mission to make a change in the world. If you're ready to Unleash yourself, set yourself FREE from limiting beliefs and create, launch & sell your unique gifts in alignment with your Human Design… This space is for YOU

www.vanessahallick.com/wild-bold-free-membership

If you can't see what you're looking for above, please visit my website www.vanessahallick.com for further information.

Free Resources

QUANTUM UPLEVEL

2 Part training and activations to support you with upleveling your life & business. If you're ready to unlock your wealth codes, speak your truth and make the income and impact you know you're meant for, click here to access these trainings:

www.vanessahallick.com/quantum-uplevel

PAID TO BE YOU

This is an exclusive portal for readers of this book with training, activation and the Rapid Energetic Recoding™ method to support you with shifting on a mental, emotional, physical and spiritual level.

www.vanessahallick.com/paid

PODCAST: PAID TO BE YOU PODCAST

This is a podcast for the visionary entrepreneur that wants to create a life and business on their terms with the impact, income and intimacy you are meant for. Vanessa, provides practical tools and advice to take your business to the next level. You will also hear from other women who share their inspirational stories and how they overcame challenges to create a business where they get Paid to be the best versions of themselves.

If you're ready to elevate abundance, speak your truth and get Paid for your unique gifts & signature methodology this is a must- listen. Available on Spotify, Stitcher, iTunes and all major podcast providers.

podcasts.apple.com/us/podcast/paid-to-be-you

SOCIAL MEDIA

Instagram: www.instagram.com/vanessabusinesscoach
Facebook: www.facebook.com/vanessa.hallick
Pinterest: pinterest.com/vanessahallick/_created